WEST COAST WHALE WATCHING

The Complete Guide
To Observing Marine Mammals

By
Richard C. Kreitman
and
Mary Jane Schram

HarperCollins*West*
An Imprint of HarperCollins*Publishers*

Illustrations by: Pieter A. Folkens
Maps by: Michael B. Blum

FIRST EDITION

Library of Congress Cataloging-in-Publication Data:
Kreitman, Richard C.
West coast whale watching : the complete guide to observing marine mammals / Richard C. Kreitman and Mary Jane Schramm.
p. cm.
Includes bibliographical references and index.
ISBN 0–06–258619–X

1. Whale watching—Pacific Coast (North America)—Guidebooks. 2. Marine mammals—Pacific Coast (North America) 3. Wildlife watching—Pacific Coast (North America)—Guidebooks. 4. Pacific Coast (North America)—Guidebooks. I. Schramm, Mary Jane. II. Title.
QL737.c4k76 1995
599.5'0979—dc20   95–7213

95 96 97 98 99 ❖ HAD 10 9 8 7 6 5 4 3 2 1

Part I: Humpback (*Megaptera novaeangliae*), mother and calf.
Part II: Sperm whale (*Physeter macrocephalus*), adult bull.
Part III: Gray whale (*Eschrichtius robustus*), cow and calf.

CONTENTS

ACKNOWLEDGMENTS

Our knowledge of marine mammals took a quantum leap forward in the past few decades, and we first wish to acknowledge those dedicated professionals and volunteers whose collective hard work make this possible. Their findings and insights, based on many thousands of hours in the field and laboratory, and built upon a foundation of earlier observations, have brought to the rest of us a better understanding of whales, seals, and their kin.

We wish to thank The Marine Mammal Center in Sausalito for the opportunity to work directly with wild marine mammals and learn firsthand the qualities that so fascinate us. Thanks also to the Gulf of the Farallones National Marine Sanctuary, for protecting and providing venues through which we can experience one of the West Coast's most extraordinary marine ecosystems. To the Point Reyes Bird Observatory, for allowing the assistance of an enthusiastic volunteer field researcher on their Farallon Islands elephant seal project; and to Oceanic Society Expeditions, for many voyages of discovery into some of the most remarkable marine mammal habitats in the world.

Individual thanks to Steve Leatherwood, for giving precious time, good counsel, and friendly encouragement for this project; to Dr. Larry Barnes, for his unique and valuable insights into cetacean evolution; to Pieter Folkens, for both his extraordinary illustrations and his knowledge of marine mammal natural history; and to many other associates who have offered suggestions, comments, and support.

Finally, we would like to thank the marine mammal boat and tour operators who cooperated with us in writing this book and who each year take hundreds of thousands of us out to view these magnificent creatures in their native habitat.

INTRODUCTION

What is it about whales that so fires the imagination and attracts the intense interest of millions of people? Part of the answer is that whales are the biggest animals that ever lived—and the giant never fails to get our attention. If all dinosaurs had been the size of chickens, children wouldn't be obsessed with them. And by being the biggest they simply have more raw living energy than any other creature. You feel that energy when you are near them.

One of my first childhood memories is of standing awestruck beneath the suspended life-size model of a blue whale in New York's American Museum of Natural History. This behemoth was far more impressive than the dinosaur skeletons in the next room, perhaps because I knew it represented a modern living animal.

Those childhood memories came back to mind on my first whale-watching trip out to the Farallon Islands off San Francisco's Golden Gate when we spotted several blue whales in the near distance. It gave me chills to see this huge creature in the flesh, the powerful, graceful, unhurried movements as it swam on the surface and then lifted its immense, dripping tail flukes just above the water before diving out of sight. When the expansive, glistening back appeared again a few minutes later and a column of vapor shot 30 feet into the air, I cheered along with everyone on board.

We cheered on this near-mythical animal, the largest in the history of life on earth, for having survived man's best attempts to eliminate it, and just for being here with us. With an estimated worldwide population of 12,000 blues, only 1,500 of which are in the North Pacific, we also rejoiced at our good fortune in seeing one.

Perhaps it is the precarious yet tenacious endurance of whales that feeds our passion. Linked to our collective guilt over the near extermination of many whale species, their existence, even in small numbers, is a kind of reassurance that we haven't destroyed the environment beyond repair. It speaks to our late awakening to the interdependence of life on earth. And while it would be premature to pat ourselves on the back, the survival of most whale populations and the remarkable recovery of our West Coast gray whale population offer some hope that we might yet save the planet.

The very *wildness* of whales draws us to them. On whale-watching excursions we see whales in their natural habitat: the vast ocean. Few of us will take an African wildlife safari, and if we do, it will likely be in a fenced and protected game reserve. But most whales live unrestricted in the limitless expanse of the world ocean, and just by boarding a whale-watching boat or standing on a Pacific Coast Highway overlook, we can view one of the earth's most magnificent creatures in its element, safe for now from the threat of extinction.

And the awesomeness of whales pervades our culture and literature, from Leviathan and the story of Jonah in the Bible to the trials of Pinocchio in the stomach of the whale to the madness of Captain Ahab in his pursuit of Moby Dick. The romance and adventure of the New England whaler is as much an archetype of the American hero as the pioneer and the cowboy.

Whales do arouse something deep within us, be it for their majestic size, their strength, their wild nature, or for reasons personal to each of us. And for all their mythic proportions, whales are remarkably accessible—going about their lives right here just a boat ride away.

That is what *West Coast Whale Watching* is about, the magnificent marine mammals—whales, dolphins, porpoises, seals, sea lions, and sea otters—that call the waters of the west coast of North America home. West Coast watchers will find some of the best whale watching in the world here, and this book is meant to serve them in two important ways. First, as a guidebook to finding the right whale-watching activity for you, listing almost 150 whale-watch cruise operators and hundreds of onshore viewing sites, from Kodiak Island in Alaska to Baja California. Second, as a field guide to help you identify the most commonly seen marine mammals along the Pacific Coast and to understand their behavior and life history.

We hope you wear out your copy carrying it with you on many future whale-watching trips and wish you good luck in finding your whales!

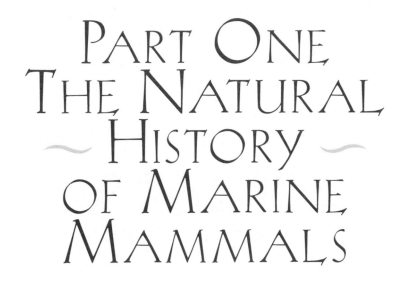

PART ONE
THE NATURAL
HISTORY
OF MARINE
MAMMALS

WHALES,
DOLPHINS,
AND
PORPOISES

Whales, dolphins, and porpoises belong to the zoological order Cetacea, a word derived from the Greek *ketos* and Latin *cetus*, meaning "big sea creature" or "whale." Cetaceans are mammals: warm-blooded, air-breathing vertebrates that give birth to live young who suckle milk from their mother's mammary glands. They are carnivorous and spend their entire lives in the water. With the exception of a few freshwater river-dwelling dolphin species, cetaceans live in the salt water of the world's seas and oceans.

Most of the approximately 78 species of cetaceans are odontocetes, or toothed whales (suborder Odontoceti). Some odontocete species have full sets of upper and lower teeth, as do most porpoises and dolphins; others, such as the sperm whale and Risso's dolphin, only have teeth in their lower jaws; while most beaked whales have only one pair of massive teeth in their lower jaw. In all, there are about 67 species of toothed whales, of which 30 or so may be seen off the west coast of North America.

Baleen whales (suborder Mysticeti) have mouths lined with baleen—flat, horny overlapping plates fringed with bristles that hang down from their upper jaws and strain food from the water. There are 11 identified species of baleen whales, 8 of which are found in West Coast waters.

Cetaceans Share the Following Features

• They breathe through blowholes atop their heads instead of through nostrils. Baleen whales have two blowholes and toothed whales have one.

• Compared with those of other mammals, cetacean jaws are stretched forward and are highly elongated.

3

- A thick layer of fat under the skin, called blubber, serves as both insulation and an energy reserve.
- Genitalia and teats are hidden in body slits, which helps streamline the body for efficient swimming.
- There are no external ears, just tiny pinholes.
- They have front flippers that are evolved from mammalian forelimbs.
- There are no external hind limbs, although vestigial hind limb bones are found embedded in the pelvic muscles of some whales.
- A muscular, laterally compressed tail, which flattens into horizontal flukes, provides forward locomotion.
- Their bodies are hairless, although all species have a few vestigial hairs, usually around blowholes and snouts, which may serve as tactile sensors.

Toothed Whales

Melon, Beak, Blowhole, Dorsal Fin, Tail Stock, Teeth, Eye, Flipper, Navel, Uro-genital Opening, Flukes

Baleen Whales

Blowhole, Eye, Rostrum, Dorsal Fin, Tail Stock, Baleen, Flipper, Flukes, Ventral Throat Grooves

How Whales Evolved

During the early Eocene epoch, around 55 million years ago, the land-dwelling mammalian ancestors of modern whales and dolphins began wetting their feet in the warm, shallow waters of ancient seas and rivers, in what is now the Mediterranean and the Arabian Gulf region. They colonized the rich ecological niche left behind when the large marine reptiles that had preyed on the ocean's fish, crustaceans, and mollusks became extinct during the great cetaceous extinction.

Pakicetus, one of the earliest identified fossil ancestors of modern whales, was discovered in Pakistan's Himalayan region in the early 1980s. The ear bones of these medium-size, four-footed carnivorous animals show adaptations for underwater hearing, so they probably led an amphibious existence. Pakicetes were related to an extinct order of hoofed land-dwelling mammals, the mesonychids, that are thought to be the ancestors of the whale's closest living mammalian relatives—modern cows, pigs, and sheep.

The first true cetaceans—members of the extinct order Archaeocetes, or "ancient whales"—appeared around 50 million years ago. Over the next 10 to 15 million years they colonized the world ocean. These creatures shared many physical characteristics with modern whales.

Among modern groups of whale species, the most ancient lineage belongs to the sperm whale family (Physeteridae), whose remains have been found in early Oligocene sediments more than 30 million years old. The right whales (family Balaenidae) entered the picture in the early Miocene, some 24 million years ago. Most other modern cetacean families, toothed and baleen, began appearing in the late Miocene, just over 10 million years ago. One puzzle is the gray whale, whose relatively primitive physiology indicates an ancient evolutionary lineage, but whose only fossil records are very recent.

As they evolved, cetacean species developed complex physiological adaptations that permitted them to colonize and thrive in the entire world ocean and in many major river systems, from the warm, shallow, muddy backwaters of the Amazon to the depths of the coldest polar seas.

Locomotion

There are accounts of harpooned right whales towing fully rigged whaling ships for hours at a time at steady speeds of 1 to 2 mph. Though enormously powerful, right whales are among the slowest of cetaceans, capable of reaching perhaps 10 to 12 mph

5

Archaeocete—generalized Durodontid, late Eocene, about forty million years ago. Note the vestigial femur protruding from the flank and the nostrils on top of the upper jaw.

under duress. When feeding, they normally travel at only 1 to 3 mph, the same as most of the great whales. When cruising or migrating, they increase their speed to a still sedate 3 to 7 mph. Gray whales, which average about 100 miles per day on their annual migrations along the West Coast, attain similar swimming speeds. Rorquals, the third family of baleen whales, are much faster swimmers. One rorqual, the sei whale, is the acknowledged champ, capable of exceeding 30 mph in a sprint, while fin whales run a close second. Except for the humpbacks, which have a top speed of about 15 mph, rorquals are capable of surpassing 20 mph. Cruising/migrating speeds for the rorquals range from 3 to 15 mph. (Consider that many large charter fishing/whale-watching boats only do about 12 to 14 mph at normal cruising speeds.)

Sperm whales, the largest of the toothed whales, have been clocked at 25 mph when harpooned, while their normal cruising speeds are around 5 mph. Orcas can attain speeds of 27 mph, and many dolphin species are capable of reaching 20 to 25 mph.

Whales and dolphins are propelled through the water by the up-and-down movement of their tail flukes, powered by massive muscles above and below the tail stock. The front flippers, evolved from mammalian forelimbs, function as stabilizers and turning mechanisms, not as paddles for propulsion.

But powerful tail flukes and streamlined bodies alone do not account for the prodigious speeds cetaceans are capable of. Whales and dolphins create a laminar (smooth and nonturbulent) flow of water over their bodies when they swim, greatly reducing friction and increasing the rate of speed. Laminar flow is created for the most part by the action of the tail flukes and is aided by several other mechanisms. One is the remarkable ability of a whale's outer layer of skin to instantaneously adjust to even slight changes in surface pressure, flexing and rippling minutely to foil turbulence and maintain efficient flow. Another is the oils found in the surface skin cells, which may reduce drag as they are sloughed off. Finally, mucous glands around the eyes produce a substance that streams back over a cetacean's body in small amounts, perhaps functioning like the mucous or slime that coats fish scales, to further lower water resistance.

Breathing and Diving

Unlike fish, which extract oxygen from water with their gills, whales and dolphins are mammals and must surface regularly to exhale and breathe in fresh air. Cetaceans are able to dive to extreme depths, hold their breath for an extended amount of time, return to the surface rapidly, and remain there for a brief period before diving again. Diving and breath-holding abilities vary widely among species.

The acknowledged cetacean deep-diving and breath-holding champions are the sperm whale and the bottlenose whale. Sperm whales have been timed in dives of 90 minutes, and regularly dive to 3,000 feet. They have been found tangled in undersea telephone cables 3,720 feet down, and evidence suggests they can dive to 10,000 feet or more. Bottlenose whales have been timed at two hours underwater, and may dive to depths equivalent to those attained by the sperm whale. The large baleen whales tend to feed close to the surface and generally have relatively short dives of 5 to 10 minutes with a maximum time submerged of about 40 minutes. Bottlenose dolphins dive for up to 15 minutes, whereas the common dolphin stays down for only 3 minutes.

One of the first evolutionary modifications that helped cetaceans adapt to their aquatic environment was the movement of the nostrils to the top of the head, where they became the blowholes. These blowholes allow whales to breathe while remaining almost entirely submerged and while swimming fast. Blowholes are blocked with nasal plugs (odontocetes) or powerful muscles (mysticetes), which open only when the whale surfaces to exhale and inhale. Whales have developed a complex series of plugs and valves that prevent water from getting into the respiratory system.

One would think that cetaceans would need enormous lung capacity to enable them to hold their breath for so long. Surprisingly, whales actually have lungs that are quite small relative to their total size. For example, human lungs on the average account for 7 percent of body weight, but no cetacean species has more than 3 percent. And the species that dive the deepest have the smallest lungs proportionally. The answer to this apparent paradox is twofold. First, the oxygen whales need to stay submerged for extended periods is not stored in their lungs but in the hemoglobin of their huge blood supply (10 to 15 percent of body weight in whales vs. 7 percent in humans) and in a hemoglobinlike substance called myoglobin in their muscles, which may account for over 40 percent of the oxygen reserves needed for a deep dive. Second, whale lungs are extremely efficient. It is estimated that whales exchange 80 to 90 percent of the air in their lungs with each breath, compared to a 10 to 15 percent exchange in humans. This is possible because cetacean lungs are elongated, with a large surface area facing a large diaphragm. Upon surfacing from a dive this powerful diaphragm forces nearly all the air out of the lungs in a fraction of a second. This explosive exhalation produces the vaporous blow, or spout, so commonly associated with whales, which in some species can be heard from a mile away.

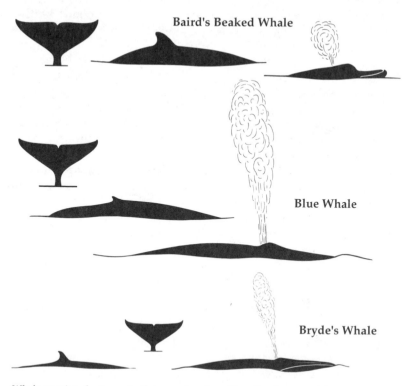

Baird's Beaked Whale

Blue Whale

Bryde's Whale

Whale spotting chart: spouts, flukes, and surface silhouettes (not to scale).

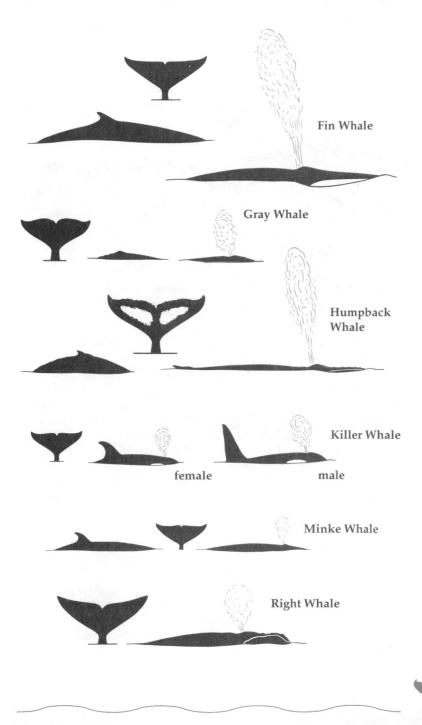

Fin Whale

Gray Whale

Humpback Whale

Killer Whale

female   male

Minke Whale

Right Whale

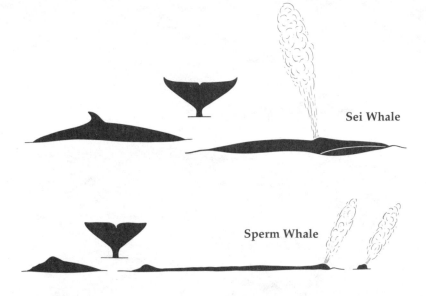

Sei Whale

Sperm Whale

The Spout

What exactly is the spout (or blow) and what makes it visible? The spout is caused by the condensation of warm, moist air as it is rapidly exhaled. In cold areas, the effect is identical to seeing your own breath on a chilly day. In warm areas, the phenomenon of adiabatic cooling (in which pressurized gas cools rapidly when released) provides enough condensation to make the blow visible. In addition to water vapor, the blow contains fine droplets of several normal mucosal secretions from the lungs and nasal passages. These may add to the visibility of the condensed vapor and account for the blow's often acrid, fishy smell. Under the right conditions the blow of a large whale can be seen for miles. It is the blow that alerts whale watchers—whether scanning the waters with binoculars from the rail of a twin diesel, or peering with the naked eye onshore—that the animals are nearby.

In the smallest baleen whales and the smaller toothed whales the blow is often inconspicuous and is not useful to us for spotting or identifying whales. But the blows of the great whales are distinct enough to permit positive identification of some species. While all baleen whales have two blowholes, only the two large right whales—the Northern right whale and the bowhead whale—have blowholes sufficiently wide apart to produce two distinct plumes of vapor in a wide V-shaped fan of mist. The gray whale's blow rises in a single column and spreads into a bushy crown, at times heart shaped. The large rorquals—blue, fin, sei, and Bryde's whales—produce single majestic columns of spray. The sperm whale's blowhole is set to the front of its huge head, and the highly distinct spout angles sharply forward and to the left. Please note that the calmer the day, the better your chances of using the blow to identify different species, as high winds can make it difficult to even see the blow.

Food and Feeding

All whales are carnivores and eat marine animals. Ironically, most of the largest whales—the great baleen whales—feed almost exclusively on floating zooplankton, among the ocean's smallest creatures. Most other whales eat squid and fish, while a few species supplement their diet with warm-blooded prey: pinnipeds, seabirds, and other cetaceans. Baleen whales and toothed whales have very distinct feeding behaviors.

Baleen whales are filter feeders, straining food from the water with the characteristic fringed baleen plates that line their mouths. The right and bowhead whales generally feed by swimming at the surface with open mouths, constantly filtering out their tiny prey and periodically closing their mouths to scrape off the accumulated food with their tongues and swallow. They live primarily off the smallest plankton species, which abound in the cold polar and subpolar seas.

The rorquals—blue, fin, Bryde's, minke, and humpback whales—are gulpers, taking large quantities of water into their expandable throats and then squeezing it out through the sides, trapping the food in the baleen. Their main food sources vary. Blue whales live almost entirely on krill, the shrimplike crustaceans that inhabit the upper, sunlit part of the water and feed on marine algae. Fin, Bryde's, minke, and humpback whales tend to eat krill and other zooplankton in the Southern Hemisphere, but in the northern Pacific prefer small fish like sardines, herring, pollack, and anchovies. One rorqual, the sei, exhibits both skimming and gulping behavior, depending on available food sources.

Then there are the bottom feeders, the gray whales, who suck up the amphipod-rich top layer of mud in the shallow Alaskan seas of their summer feeding grounds. Their huge tongue forces the water and mud out of the mouth, trapping the small crustaceans in the baleen.

Toothed whales grasp and swallow their food, which consists mainly of squid and fish, and for some species, mollusks and crustaceans. At least one species, the well-known orca, or killer whale, eats warm-blooded prey. While the resident pods of the Puget

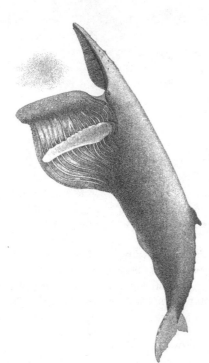

Typical rorqual feeding behavior: a humpback whale about to engulf a school of small fish. Note the baleen plates hanging from the upper jaw.

Sound in the Northwest eat salmon almost exclusively—others regularly feed on seals, sea lions, penguins, sea turtles, and small cetaceans such as dolphins and porpoises. In groups they have been known to attack and kill larger whales, up to and including blue and sperm whales. Some related species, like the false killer whale, have attacked dolphins and young humpback whales.

The oceanic dolphins are largely fish and squid eaters, and have evolved long jaws filled with tiny, sharp teeth adapted to grabbing small, fast-moving prey one at a time. Their diets vary according to season and location. Common dolphins off the southern California coast eat mainly squid and anchovies during the winter. In the summer they switch to smelt and lantern fish. A few dolphin species supplement their diet with shrimp and other crustaceans. Porpoises have similar diets.

Some of the toothed whales are almost exclusively squid eaters. The best known of these is the sperm whale, the largest toothed whale, which dives thousands of feet to hunt giant squid, which can be over 40 feet long. When closer inshore, sperm whales modify their diets and eat more fish. Bottlenose and pilot whales also live mainly on squid but have been known to supplement that with small fish such as herring.

Staying Warm

As warm-blooded mammals, whales must maintain their body temperature at a steady level while living in a watery world that absorbs heat much faster than air does. The average body temperature of whales is a very familiar 98.6°F, whether they are in the warm surface waters of the tropics or the coldest ocean depths and polar seas.

Blubber, the thick blanket of fat in the lower level of skin, acts as an insulating layer to conserve body heat and store energy. The whale's nearly cylindrical body has few appendages, minimizing the heat-exchanging surface area relative to body weight. The bigger a whale is, the lower this critical ratio becomes. The huge, rotund bowhead whale, which inhabits the most frigid of polar seas, may have the lowest area-to-weight ratio of all. Appropriately, bowheads have the thickest blubber, up to 20 inches thick. An extremely effective insulator, this blubber is laced with a network of capillaries and arteries that can minimize heat loss or maximize heat exchange.

Cetaceans have also developed a circulatory system that utilizes an efficient method of heat exchange, in which arteries running out to extremities are surrounded by a web of veins that carry blood back toward the heart. The warm arterial blood gradually exchanges heat with the cool venous blood as it gets farther from the heart and closer to the fins and flukes, where the potential for heat loss is greatest. Called "countercurrent heat exchange," this process occurs in many mammals, including humans, but not as efficiently as with whales.

The Sense of Touch

Whales and dolphins have a very highly developed sense of touch. Divers swimming with great whales have reported that the touch of a single finger can cause the whole animal to shudder. Whales themselves employ touch most overtly in sexual and social contact, spending a good part of the day touching and caressing with flippers, rubbing their bodies against each other, and pressing against one another with their genitals (often regardless of gender or species). Mothers are constantly coaxing, caressing, prodding, and fondling their calves.

Whale skin is highly sensitive to small changes in pressure, allowing the animal to adjust its surface shape minutely to accommodate changes in turbulence and thus maintain efficient laminar flow. Similarly, whales and dolphins are able to sense wave pressure, such as that caused by moving vessels, and position themselves to bow ride. Baby whales make use of this sense to ride on the pressure waves created by their swimming mothers, permitting them to keep up without growing exhausted.

Baby humpback hitching a ride on its swimming mother's pressure wave.

Especially sensitive skin around the blowhole may detect the boundary between water and air, and trigger the opening of the blowhole. In some whale species, vestigial hairs or whiskers, called vibrissae, found on the top of the head and on the chin apparently serve the same purpose, as there are a large number of nerve endings around the follicles making them highly sensitive to touch. Chin whiskers may be important sense organs for the river-dwelling cetaceans who live in murky, muddy waters.

Vision

Cetaceans have extraordinary vision, which must function in a wider range of visual environments than that of land-dwelling mammals. The whale's eye must work in the full sunlight and air above the surface, in the brightly lit water just beneath the surface, and in the cold, dark ocean deep, where water pressures are extreme. This wide range of function is attained by having an elliptical rather than spherical eye with a large pupil and a very strong set of surrounding muscles that can alter the shape of the lens to focus both in water and in the air. Large pupils gather light in the dim depths and can be reduced to mere slits in bright surface light.

Mucous-secreting glands under the upper eyelid shield the pupil from seawater, and thick eye walls protect it from pressure.

The eyes of large baleen whales and the sperm whale are set so far apart on either side of the head that it is unlikely they have stereoscopic vision when looking forward. Due to the placement of their eyes at the corners of their jaws, baleen whales, when their mouths are agape, may be able to see the prey they are about to engulf. The smaller toothed whales and dolphins do have binocular vision, though direction and strength vary among species. Bottlenose dolphins are able to independently focus and move their two eyes, as well as adjust for light—a useful adaptation for an animal who often swims on its side, looking up at the sky and into the depths at the same time.

Hearing and Communication

Water transmits sound five times faster than air does and over much greater distances. Physiological adaptations have made hearing the whale's most highly refined sense. Used both for communication and, in toothed whales, for echolocation (the process of finding and distinguishing objects using sound waves), the sense of hearing is what enables many whales to "see" their world most clearly.

Paradoxically, whales lack external ears and instead have pinhole-size openings just behind the eyes. These are connected to constricted auditory canals, which in baleen whales are blocked by tissue and solid wax plugs. How do whales hear, if not through their ears? Specialized bones in their skull and jaws transmit sound to the inner ear. It appears that toothed whales with the most sensitive echolocation abilities may receive the returning sound waves from their own echolocation clicks through specially adapted oil deposits in their lower jaws and connected to the inner ear by a structure known as the acoustic window.

The echolocation clicks of toothed whales are usually above 20,000 Hz (cycles per second) and can reach as high as 300,000 Hz (the upper limit of human hearing is about 25,000 Hz). These sounds function like the sonar used by bats and human sonic detection devices, providing the whales with incredibly detailed information about the size, location, shape, and composition of objects. There is so much energy in some of these sounds that evidence suggests that certain toothed whale species can and do use the clicks to stun their prey: small fish and squid. There is no evidence that baleen whales echolocate.

In the early 1950s the U.S. Navy put its SOFAR system of long-range undersea listening stations into operation. In many ocean

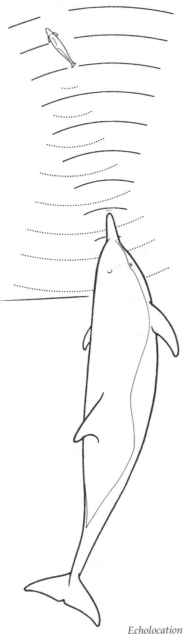

Echolocation in dolphins.

regions they found a loud, steady low-frequency hum of 20 Hz, so steady that they thought it must come from a mechanical source. As it turned out, fin whales made the sounds.

It is believed that the high-energy, low-frequency sounds (15 to 3,000 Hz) made by large baleen whales are used in communication. These sounds carry great distances underwater, and if emitted into certain deep ocean channels that focus and carry them efficiently, they could presumably be heard thousands of miles away. In today's noisy oceans, filled with boats and other noisy mechanical devices, the effective range of such communication, if it exists, would be drastically shortened but could still be scores or even hundreds of miles. Some speculate that the great baleen whales stay in contact over vast distances using these low frequencies. If so, we may have an incorrect view of species like the blue whale, who are thought to be solitary or prone to traveling in groups of two or three individuals. In reality they might live in and maintain communication with much larger groups—only these groups are spread out over hundreds or thousands of square miles of ocean.

In addition to these low-frequency moans, both baleen and toothed whales produce a wide range of grunts, clicks, chirps, whistles, thumps, and belches, all generally under 15,000 Hz in frequency, which also appear to function as a form of communication within groups. The songs of the humpback whale fall into this category.

Biomagnetism

Biomagnetism, a fairly new area of study, explores the notion that many organisms have a sensory ability to detect the earth's magnetic field. Tiny concentrations of magnetite, magnetic crystals of iron oxide, have been found in bacteria, insects, fish, birds, and mammals. These crystals may act as biological compasses, aiding in long-distance navigation. Among cetaceans, magnetite has been found in the brains of Dall's porpoises, common dolphins, humpback whales, Cuvier's beaked whales, and other species.

Some people believe cetaceans are well endowed with this biomagnetic sense. While the normal geomagnetic lines of the earth have a north-south orientation, geomagnetic anomalies exist in areas of seamounts, mid-ocean rift zones and trenches, and along continental shelves. If whales are sensitive enough to recognize such zones, they would have a geomagnetic road map of the open sea. Whales often become stranded in shallow waters, and there is strong evidence to suggest that in many cases local coastal distortions in the geomagnetic field had confused their navigational abilities.

Family Life

In a scenario repeated thousands of times each year, a female whale or dolphin, heavy with calf and about to give birth, is swimming slowly near the surface of some tropical sea, attended by one or more mature females of her species. As the calf emerges into its welcoming but perilous ocean world, one of these "aunts" approaches gently and using her flipper guides the newborn to the surface for its first breath of air. Even though whales are excellent mothers who are nurturing and protective of their young, in many species the aunt will continue to help the mother shield the calf from danger, will baby-sit when she is off foraging for food, and will assist a sick calf by supporting it at the surface.

Most toothed whales and dolphins are social animals, living in groups that share in courtship and breeding, raising their young, finding food, and defending against predators. The helpful aunt just described is demonstrating typical caregiving whale behavior. While cetaceans aren't the only order of mammals that exhibit such behaviors, the level at which they do it and the fact that they do it for individuals outside their own kinship groups, even outside their own species, are most impressive. It is one reason why whales are so appealing to so many people, and it even impressed the whalers who exploited this animal's loyalty to kin and kind in order to increase their slaughter.

THE NATURAL HISTORY OF MARINE MAMMALS

All cetaceans, whales and dolphins included, produce only single offspring, with twins a very rare occurence. For many species mating and birth are restricted to specific seasons, tied to annual cycles of food availability or the annual migrations from summer feeding grounds to winter breeding and calving grounds.

Some species, notably the gray whale, have traditional calving grounds where virtually the entire population migrates each year and where pregnant females give birth. For many of the great whales, almost nothing is known of their breeding and calving habits and locations. They apparently move to isolated offshore areas to calve.

In the large baleen whales, conception usually occurs in the winter and birth comes 10 to 14 months later, when the mothers are back in warmer winter grounds. Calves are typically weaned in anywhere from 6 months to a year, and females generally give birth every second or third year. The age of sexual maturity varies from 4 to 10 years.

Toothed whales also tend to conceive in definite seasons, but these vary by species. Gestation periods are variable, with some in the 11- to 12-month range and others up to 17 months. For sperm whales it may be as long as 19 months. Weaning ages and the time between births tend to be much longer than for baleen whales. Some mothers suckle their calves for several years.

Courtship and mating behavior varies by species. Some toothed whales, including the sperm whale, have polygynous mating systems, where one adult male maintains a "harem" of females over some period of time and fights off any male that tries to intrude. Most baleen whales, on the other hand, are promiscuous, with males competing for individual females, and females sometimes mating with multiple partners. Humpback males try to monopolize a single female, leading to aggressive behavior and the occasional fight. Gray, bowhead, and right whale females mate with multiple partners, and males show little or no aggression toward each other. Sex in these species often involves a threesome, with a second male helping out by wedging his body against the female to keep her in position.

For many of the smaller whales and dolphins, particularly those observed in captivity, sex is a favorite and frequent activity. In all whales, sex usually involves a lot of display behavior and play, with partners rubbing against each other and stroking each other with their fins. The most common mating position has the female face-down at the surface and the male gliding beneath, belly up.

2

PINNIPEDS AND SEA OTTERS

Pinnipeds

Pinnipeds, a word derived from the Latin *pinnae* and *pedis,* meaning "feather" and "footed," are fin-footed sea mammals who are not completely adapted to a marine environment. Unlike cetaceans, pinnipeds retained their hairy coats. And their four limbs became flippers that are webbed to give them speed and strength in swimming. They have short, muscular, highly streamlined bodies. Their large eyes and sensitive whiskers, called vibrissae, enable them to locate food—mostly fish and squid—in the murky, nutrient-rich ocean depths. To maintain a warm body temperature in near-freezing water, they developed a layer of blubber. This blubber layer is thickest in Arctic seals and relatively thin in fur seals, whose dense underfur provides insulation. Fur density among fur seals can reach over 360,000 hairs per square inch.

As the forebears of the modern pinniped became adapted to an amphibious existence they developed unique physiological adaptations to an aquatic environment, yet remained tied to the land for breeding and birthing purposes. Some species spend nearly their entire lives foraging at sea, returning to land only to molt, mate, give birth, and rear their young. The remains of primitive pinnipeds and an otterlike pinniped (which may be a "missing link" between the terrestrial ancestors of bears and some sea lions) were found in California's San Juan Valley and date back to the early Miocene, about 23 million years ago.

Seals and sea lions, like all life forms, are primarily driven by one urge: the need to breed and thus ensure the continuation of the species. They can be found in a wide variety of habitats; they exhibit vastly different feeding and breeding strategies; and they follow various migration patterns. Several species may live in the same area at one time, as they do on California's Farallon Islands and Channel Islands, and their myriad shapes, sizes, and behaviors make them fascinating subjects for observation.

Habitats range from rugged sea-battered coasts and offshore islands to gently sloping sandy beaches to frigid ice shelves. On land their principal need is to remain isolated from predators and other disturbances, including humans. At sea they frequent various ocean zones, from shallow nearshore waters over the continental shelf to deep seas hundreds of miles from land, sometimes diving to depths of over 5,000 feet. Some species, such as harbor seals, remain in one general region throughout their lives, while others may migrate thousands of miles each year through both temperate and tropical habitats, in the ocean and along the coast.

Pinnipeds need accessible places where they can haul out to rest, molt, give birth, and, in some species, mate. They require a reliable and abundant food source and will congregate around areas of high productivity, such as submarine canyons and seamounts, banks, and river mouths in temperate regions, and at the edge of the polar ice sheet. A few species, including the monk seal, inhabit tropical waters. But warmer waters are generally nutrient poor and cannot support large resident populations.

Seal migration varies considerably from species to species. Those seals that do migrate are driven largely by the need to feed and the need to reproduce. The Northern fur seal and other species migrate many thousands of miles each year, while harbor seals may remain within a few miles of their birthplace. Most seal species show site fidelity, meaning they return faithfully to the same location, known as a rookery, for breeding or molting, at times even in the face of danger. This predictability, which made it easy for hunters to descend on seal breeding grounds in the past, now allows scientists to closely observe seal behavior on the rookeries and to employ such technical innovations as radiotagging and satellite tracking to monitor their movements in the water.

Pinnipeds feed upon a variety of seafood—from bony fish and squid to crustaceans—and have been known to sample the occasional bird or small seal. Their teeth are designed for grabbing, holding, and tearing but not for chewing. Small prey are usually swallowed whole. Sea lions often toss fish into the air playfully before actually downing them; in fact, they've been observed playing Frisbee with disk-shaped ocean sunfish.

Some seal species can fast for months. Northern elephant seals spend their entire breeding season hauled out, living off accumulated fat stores and oxidizing their blubber into water. They may lose up to a third of their body weight by the end of this strenuous fast. This behavior allows them to keep their place in the breeding colony. After the breeding season, they return to sea to forage for several months before hauling out again.

Most pinnipeds breed at the same time each year. Females (cows) have a two-horned uterus that enables them to mate soon after giving birth. Single pups are born at the rookeries (twin births are rare).

Maternal involvement in pup rearing can range from minimal to intensive, and nurturing strategies vary widely among species. But all female pinnipeds are devoted mothers, each in the manner of her species. Seal milk is extremely rich in fat (up to 55 percent), and the pups gain weight rapidly.

An elephant seal will nurse her pup for 28 to 30 days without ever leaving its side, going without food the entire time. Weaning occurs abruptly in this species when the pup has quadrupled its birth weight. By then, the cow will have lost one-third of her own weight. She must return to the sea immediately to replenish fat stores and regain her health in preparation for her new pregnancy. She does not teach her pup how to swim or forage for food. Her month-old pup, or "weaner," will live off accumulated fat until it learns to forage successfully, largely through trial and error.

Other species, such as harbor seals, will often look for food between nursing bouts, leaving their pups on the shore, then wean them after four to six weeks. Sea lions and fur seals do the same, but they may nurse their pups for a year or more. Some swim with their pups, demonstrate feeding techniques, and generally orient them to their environment. The male seal's reproductive role requires him to mate and pass along his genes, but he doesn't participate in pup rearing.

Most pinnipeds feed near the surface. Others can dive to depths of over 5,000 feet for a duration of two hours, surfacing only briefly before the next dive. To survive the tremendous pressures of the deep and to conserve oxygen, pinnipeds, like cetaceans, have evolved a number of remarkable physical adaptations. When a pinniped dives it exhales, its heartbeat slows, and blood vessels near the skin constrict, shunting the blood to vital organs such as the heart and brain. Oxygen is stored in the blood, muscles, and lung tissues, and its consumption is cut by a third.

History of Exploitation

Most species of pinnipeds have been exploited by humans for their fur, flesh, meat, and oil. Commercial hunting of the Northern fur seal in Alaska's Pribilof Islands began in the late 18th century, both on the breeding rookeries and at sea. Millions of animals died in the ensuing decades of unregulated slaughter until the population of fur seals collapsed. Another species that was intensively hunted is the Northern elephant seal. When Yankee whalers hunted the gray whale to commercial extinction along the California coast, they turned to the elephant seal as an alternate source of oil, which could be rendered from the animal's thick blubber. No longer did they need to take to the seas to do battle with Leviathan; elephant seals could be found on the breeding grounds to which they returned faithfully year after year, along the California coast and offshore islands, south to Baja California. There they were easy targets and simply had to be corralled and lanced. By 1880 the elephant seal was believed to be extinct; then scientists from the Smithsonian Institution discovered a small population on remote

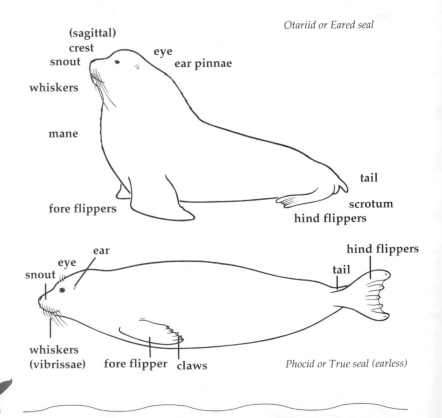

Otariid or Eared seal

(sagittal)
crest
snout
eye
ear pinnae
whiskers
mane
tail
fore flippers
scrotum
hind flippers

ear
hind flippers
eye
snout
tail
whiskers
(vibrissae)
fore flipper
claws

Phocid or True seal (earless)

Guadalupe Island off northern Baja and killed most of them for scientific specimens. Elephant seals are now protected by the Marine Mammal Protection Act and by Mexican law. The 1991 population was estimated at nearly 120,000. Limited numbers of nonbreeding fur seals are currently being hunted at rookeries under the supervision of the U.S. Fisheries Service. Permission for pelagic hunting (in the ocean) is granted only to aborigines, who use primitive methods and hunt only on a subsistence basis.

Sea Otters

The sea otter is a carnivore and a member of the weasel family (Mustelidae), which also includes the mink, marten, badger, skunk, wolverine, and other otters. Fossil records indicate that the first otters appeared some 30 million years ago and from these, sea otters branched off about 5 to 7 million years ago. The northern Pacific population became isolated about 2 million years ago.

Sea otters have the densest and most luxurious fur of any animal on earth, a distinction that led to the near extinction of the species. Some parts of a sea otter's body are covered with up to a million hairs per square inch. (Compare that to humans, who average 100,000 hairs per head.) Unlike cetaceans and pinnipeds, sea otters do not have a layer of blubber to provide insulation and buoyancy. Instead, it is this extraordinarily dense and water-resistant fur that enables them to stay warm and afloat in frigid water. Air bubbles trapped in the fur do the job. To keep their fur dry and aerated, sea otters devote a good part of each day to cleaning and grooming.

From this dense coat of inch-long underhairs protrude guard hairs, which are up to a half-inch longer. For every guard hair there are 60 to 80 underhairs bundled together in a follicle. These guard hairs make up the otter's soft and fluffy outercoat. They protect and support the fine undercoat by lying flat when the animal is under water to provide a waterproof blanket. If the coat gets dirty or oily, the animal becomes waterlogged and will probably freeze to death. This makes sea otters especially vulnerable to man-made pollution, particularly oil spills. After the Exxon *Valdez* ran aground in Prince William Sound in 1989, thousands of otters died.

Observe a sea otter who's just finished a long nap or a meal and the odds are you will witness a furious bout of grooming. Using both the fore and hind paws, they meticulously attend to every square inch of fur: licking, stroking, pawing, pulling, and squeezing. A master contortionist, the otter twists around, rolls, turns somersaults, and at times appears to rotate inside its own skin, which has been described as an ill-fitting suit that's several sizes too

23

large—all in pursuit of grooming those hard-to-reach spots. Afterward, the otter may turn on its stomach and blow air into the fur, or beat the water to a foamy froth with its forepaws, producing bubbles to trap in the fur. When the fur is clean and fluffed with air, the otter rides noticeably higher in the water.

Mother otters spend a lot of time grooming their pups; one was observed tending to her newborn's fur for two and a half hours straight. If they didn't do this regularly, a pup would soon get waterlogged and freeze to death. Pups start learning to groom themselves in their first month and are nearly self-sufficient in two to three months. Otters also use their thinly furred paws to regulate body temperature. When they float on their backs with paws and flippers in the air, they're not trying to be cute; completely immersing themselves in the water would greatly increase heat loss. In warmer waters or when overheated, otters will keep their paws down and transfer heat accordingly.

Sea otter fur is usually deep brown with silvery specks, but comes in various shades, from grayish or yellowish brown to nearly black. During the days of the fur trade in the eighteenth and nineteenth centuries, the blacker pelts marked with evenly distributed silver tips were the most valuable. Stomach hair tends to be lighter than back hair, while the lightest hair is on the neck and head. As sea otters age, their hair loses its pigment. Older animals take on a grizzled appearance, with some turning nearly white.

In addition to their remarkable coats, sea otters developed several other traits that enabled them to adapt to an aquatic environment. Hind paws were modified into long webbed paws that became large and powerful flippers. Lung capacity increased to two and a half times that of a similarly sized land mammal, permitting them to hold their breath on dives of up to five minutes. Changes in their blood chemistry and cardiovascular system further improved diving efficiency.

Because sea otters spend their entire lives in the ocean with no access to freshwater, they have also developed large and efficient kidneys that eliminate salt from their blood and excrete highly concentrated urea.

Sea otters have a metabolism rate that is two or three times that of land mammals, requiring them to eat up to one-third of their body weight daily. They eat a varied diet, which includes sea urchins, abalone, crab, octopus, mussels, clams, oysters, snails, starfish, innkeeper worms, fish, and squid. California otters rarely eat fish, but fish is a staple in Alaskan waters, where otter populations are very large and have been established for some time.

Individuals are very particular about what foods they eat. Studies of the world-famous otters who live along Monterey's shoreline have shown that an otter may dine on just one or two items: "Nosebuster" eats almost nothing but turban snails; "Suckerface" prefers octopus but also munches on turban snails and purple sea urchins; Female #508 is another octopus aficionada, whereas Female #182 prefers mussels and abalone.

Researchers are finding that dietary preferences and the personalized techniques for finding food are passed down from mothers to their pups. This finickiness and specialized behavior may make sense when seen in an evolutionary light: as each otter family concentrates on a different food source, over-competition in established living areas is avoided.

Given a choice, otters would probably prefer to eat abalone, sea urchins, and rock crabs. These foods are rich in nutrients and are the first things otters go for when colonizing new areas. This has put them in direct competition with fishermen, particularly abalone divers.

When otters colonize a new area, they make a dramatic impact on the local marine environment. As otters have moved along the coast repopulating their former range in recent years, there have been excellent opportunities to study this effect. Sea urchins and abalone feed on marine plants, particularly kelp, and when their populations go unchecked they keep nearshore waters free of kelp. Otters will immediately reduce the sea urchin and abalone populations, and within a few short years the kelp begins to grow into the thick underwater forests common to many parts of the West Coast. This nutrient-rich environment provides a haven for a profusion of plant and animal species.

A sea otter's jaws, much more powerful than those of their land-dwelling otter cousins, permit them to crack open the hard shells and carapaces of much of their prey. But in a unique and charming bit of behavior they also use tools to catch and eat food, something no other mammal does, primates excepted. A sea otter will dive, pick up a rock, and use it to smash or pry loose a sea urchin or abalone from where it's anchored. When they find hard-shelled foods such as a clam, they will carry a rock to the surface, place it on their chest, and repeatedly smash the clam until it breaks—and then eat it off the rock.

A mother and her pup comprise the primary sea otter social group. Males take no part in raising the young. Sea otters are usually found in groups, called pods or rafts, of from 20 to several hundred animals. Perhaps the largest pod seen in recent decades was in Bristol Bay, Alaska: 2,000 strong. Despite the fact that they live in groups, sea otters aren't very sociable—that is, there isn't much group interaction. They probably congregate in certain areas simply because these places are protected from waves and currents, making them ideal for feeding and resting. Most rafts living inshore tend to be made up of females and cubs, while all-male rafts are typically found in more exposed locations. Home ranges can be fairly wide and may overlap those of adjacent rafts. Except for a few lone males, sea otters do not defend their territory.

It appears that the territoriality of those lone males is a kind of breeding strategy. They let other males pass through but will harass those who try to forage. Any passing female will be aggressively approached to see if she is willing to mate. These males are the only sea otters who have been observed picking fights, and it's usually with each other.

Sea otters mate randomly. The male approaches the female and tries to rub or embrace her. If unwilling, she rejects him with a push or a snap, a clear brush-off. If she's willing, prior to mating they will roll around and frolic for a while, chasing each other and swimming together. Afterward, they usually form a brief but tight pair-bond and will remain together for a period of one day to over a week, sleeping, eating, and grooming together while mating frequently.

The mating position has the female on her back and the male underneath. The broad base of her tail makes rear mounting difficult, forcing him to twist around her body. To hang on during the act, the male often grips the female's nose with his teeth. Mated females often have bloody, scarred noses. When pregnant, the female ends the pair-bond, and it is unlikely this same pair will ever mate together again.

Gestation lasts anywhere from four months to a year, which sounds strange but is common among members of the weasel family, as implantation of the fertilized egg may be delayed several months. Single pups, averaging four pounds, are born at sea, although births occasionally occur on the beach. In the rare case of twin births, the mother always abandons one of the pups.

Aleutian Island and other Alaskan sea otters give birth at any time, with the heaviest concentration from April to June. Most

California sea otters are born between December and February. The pup mortality rate is high everywhere, topping out near 50 percent in Alaska due to predators and harsh winter conditions.

History of Exploitation

Archaeological remains from middens found in California and Alaska show that sea otters were hunted by aboriginal peoples for millennia, both for their meat and their fur. Some evidence suggests that these peoples may have hunted otters heavily, greatly reducing their numbers in areas close to their settlements. But in the late 18th century, when fur traders from America, Europe, and Russia discovered the sea otter populations of the northeastern Pacific, there were still scores of thousands of animals living in colonies stretching from the western Aleutian Islands to the coast of Baja California. Commercial hunting of sea otters by Russian fur traders began in the 1740s, and the sea otter populations of island after island in the Arctic seas were steadily eliminated. By 1783 the Russians had established a base on Kodiak Island in Alaska, and in 1812 founded Fort Russ (later Fort Ross) in California, north of the Golden Gate. The slaughter of sea otters and fur seals continued unabated along the entire coast until local populations were wiped out. When the Russians sold Alaska to the Americans in 1867, they thought the sea otters had been effectively eliminated. But American hunters took almost 100,000 pelts out in the following decades.

By 1911, some estimates had a total of only 500 to 1,000 sea otters left alive in a few small colonies from northern Japan to central California. In 1911 an international protective Fur Seal Treaty was signed, protecting otters, and in 1913 similar protective legislation was made federal law in the United States. Poaching remained a problem during the early decades of the 20th century, although eventually the remnant colonies began to grow. In 1972 the Marine Mammal Protection Act gave sea otters full protection in the United States.

PART TWO
WATCHING
~ WHALES ~

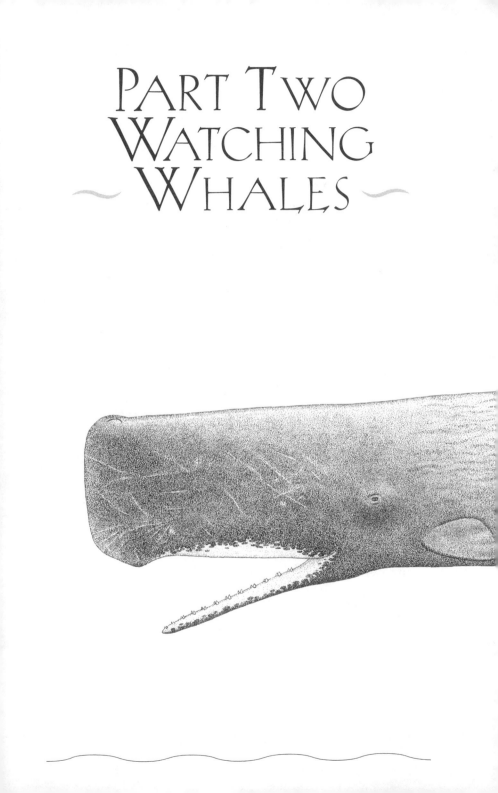

3

THE BEST WAY
TO WATCH
WHALES

What's the best way to watch whales? The short answer is: with patience and an appreciation for the majesty of the sea and all that dwells therein. That way, if the whales fail to show, you won't be completely disappointed.

Most whale watchers understand that trying to observe wild creatures in their natural habitat is anything but a sure bet. Fortunately for those impatient and single-minded types who simply *must* see a whale, the West Coast provides the closest thing to a "can't miss" opportunity to be found anywhere in the world. During the annual gray whale migration along the California coast, so many whales pass through (well over 20,000 at last count) and their appearance is so dependable in the peak seasons, that many southern California whale-watching operators offer "whale checks" good for a free trip if whales aren't encountered. If you're interested in getting such a guarantee, be sure to read the fine print: some operators count any cetacean as a whale, so if a dolphin is spotted, the trip is an official success.

Then there are those of us who get a thrill simply by being out on the water, with no objectives beyond delighting in the day and observing whatever marine wildlife we encounter. That is why *West Coast Whale Watching* covers more than just whales, and has descriptions of most of the marine mammal species that one might see on a marine natural history trip along the North American West Coast, including dolphins, porpoises, pinnipeds, and sea otters.

How to Pick a Trip

This book covers the West Coast from Kodiak Island in Alaska to the southern end of Baja California, and the Sea of Cortez between Baja and the Mexican mainland. The trips featured herein last from one and a half hours to over two weeks; cost between $10 and $7,000; and involve every mode of transportation from sea kayaks to Holland America Line luxury liners. Obviously you'll have to make some decisions early on in the process. Only you can determine what region to try, the appropriate duration of your trip, how much money to spend, and what time of the year to go. This chapter examines some of the questions you should ask yourself and any potential cruise operator. It also reviews the various types of whale-watching vessels, including their pros and cons.

Are You Taking the Kids?

Most children love whales, or at least the idea of whales. But it's one thing to look at pictures of these behemoths, and another to be trapped all day on a cold, tossing boat with a bunch of intense adults, waiting for a whale sighting that might turn out to be a brief glimpse of spouts, backs, and flukes. Each of us knows how much our children can take and how well we can control them. Please take mercy on other passengers; a whale-watching boat is not a theater that you can leave if a child gets unruly. And boats present real dangers, so be prepared to keep a very close eye on your child. (This may be one of those situations where a leash is appropriate.) If you do decide to take the kids, a short trip on a large boat is probably the best way to go, until they have demonstrated the patience and maturity necessary to handle longer voyages without driving you, the crew, and the other passengers crazy.

In areas blessed with calm waters, such as many of the locations in southeast Alaska, a good alternative for families is to charter a small six-passenger boat. Some operators prefer not to take young children on their larger boats, in deference to the other paying passengers, and will arrange a family charter on a smaller craft. Feel free to negotiate a good family rate if you take this course.

Many operators offer reduced fares for children and allow the very young to ride for free, while others provide no discount and have a minimum age requirement. Ask before you make your reservations.

What Is a Naturalist?

Some of the operators listed in this book provide naturalists who accompany and narrate some or all of their trips. Other trips are narrated by an experienced captain or crew. The reader should be aware that the experience levels of these naturalists vary widely. At one end of the scale are the trained zoologists, research biologists, and professional scientists whose lives and careers are dedicated to studying and teaching about the natural world. At the other end are the well-meaning amateur volunteers who have taken a six-hour orientation course from a museum or similar organization. They often know less than the skippers and crews who have studied the literature on their own and who have learned a lot from years of taking people out whale watching and from scientists who have been on their boats.

We have tried to note those operators who provide professional and experienced naturalists on their cruises. If having a naturalist on board is important to you, ask when you call for reservations. Regardless of whether or not the trip is narrated, you'll get the most out of it if you study on your own before you set sail. *West Coast Whale Watching* provides a very modest introduction to the subject; consider reading some of the more comprehensive works mentioned in the "Reading List" at the end of the book.

Can I Whale Watch in a Wheelchair?

Most operators can accommodate passengers in wheelchairs, on both fishing and whale-watching trips. Some provide ramps for easy boarding. In most cases, the crew will carry the passenger and the wheelchair aboard. On most boats toilets present a problem, as bulkheads and narrow doors preclude wheelchair access. Generally speaking, the larger the vessel the easier the trip is for wheelchair passengers. We have noted the few operators who are fully wheelchair accessible. Others are planning to modify their boats in the future.

Hydrophones, Anyone?

A few vessels are equipped with hydrophones, submersible microphones that can pick up whale vocalizations. This can be quite exciting around voluble species such as orcas, dolphins, and humpbacks. Some operators will even make a recording for you to take home. An onboard hydrophone is a good indicator that the operator is serious about whale watching and not just filling in time between fishing charters.

How Are the Boats Licensed?

The captains of all boats that carry paying passengers must be licensed by the Coast Guard and are subject to annual and random drug testing. The boats themselves fall into two categories: those licensed for six or fewer passengers and those licensed for seven or more. The larger boats are inspected by the Coast Guard at least once a year and are required to have a full complement of safety devices. If they conform to the rules, the Coast Guard issues them a certificate. Smaller boats are required to carry Coast Guard–approved flotation devices and basic safety equipment. Pending legislation would require the small craft to be subjected to annual inspections.

Many of the smaller operators listed in this book have voluntarily requested a Coast Guard inspection of their six-passenger boats and have a certificate to show they passed muster. In California, all commercial charter boats must also carry insurance.

To the best of our knowledge, all the boats and captains listed in this book are properly licensed and certificated, but we make no such guarantee. If this concerns you, feel free to ask any operator about his or her licensing, insurance, and inspections.

Types of Whale-Watching Operations

Sea Kayaks

With the water just inches away, sea kayaks provide a very intimate whale-watching outing. Seeing whales up close at water level is a thrilling experience, but be forewarned: as a kayaker paddling your own boat you can't count on getting close to the whales with the same assurance that motorized craft provide.

A few operators offer half- or full-day kayaking excursions (for example, Sea Quest Expeditions out of Friday Harbor, Washington), while most provide multi-day kayaking/camping trips. All of these trips are designed for a moderately fit person, not trained athletes. Travel is in wide, stable, two-person ocean kayaks; paddling is kept to a reasonable pace and duration; and anyone in good health should be able to participate. It only takes a short time to pick up the technique, and rollover training is not required.

Comfortable campsites with wall tents and cots are the typical accommodations, and most operators take pride in providing delicious hot meals. The standard trip has from 8 to 10 guests accompanied by two naturalists/guides, making for a very private experience. Operators supply varying amounts of equipment; some include outerwear, boots, gloves, and sleeping bags, while others expect clients to bring their own gear. Ask when booking.

Zodiacs and Boston Whalers

These are small, fast, open-air boats, usually in the 18- to 24-foot range. Zodiacs are the rigid, inflatable outboard-powered craft popularized by Jacques Cousteau. Boston Whalers are similar, but they have a solid fiberglass or aluminum hull. These boats can travel two to three times faster than many large cruise boats, giving them a much greater range.

A tour on one of these boats promises to be exciting, with huge helpings of cold, fresh air and salt spray. But this is not an experience for the faint of heart, people with back problems, or pregnant women. Nor is it good for the incontinent, as there are no heads (toilets) on board. The trips usually last from two to three hours, and all operators provide waterproof flotation cruiser suits, while some throw in gloves and hats.

Many of the larger expedition cruise ships have Zodiacs on board, so they can take passengers closer to the wildlife in the water and on shore.

Small Cabin Cruisers

This category includes the smaller motor vessels with enclosed cabins that are limited by the Coast Guard to carrying no more than six passengers. Most are available on a private charter basis, and some schedule trips regularly. Because of their size, they offer more flexibility in scheduling, destination, and duration. In rougher waters these boats can be quite uncomfortable, but in protected inland coastal waters they are ideal, particularly for families. Some operators are charter fishing captains who run the occasional wildlife/whale-watching trip, while others are experienced naturalists and professional biologists. Speaking of fishing, on boats like these you can often drop a line in the water to catch some salmon while you're enjoying several hours of dedicated nature watching.

Charter Sportfishing Boats

Many of the boats listed in this book are described as charter boats, by which we mean boats that are designed for charter fishing. Indeed, many belong primarily to charter fishing operations that squeeze in whale-watching trips during peak seasons or after the morning fishing charters have returned. These boats provide the best values around, such as the two- and three-hour gray whale migration cruises out of Monterey and San Diego that run $10 to $15 per person. Most are wide, seaworthy vessels with a small enclosed cabin surrounded by a one-level deck. When filled to their Coast Guard–approved capacity they can be a bit crowded, particularly when everyone flocks to the same rail to get a look at the whales off that quarter.

Long-Distance Charter Fishing Boats

These vessels are used for the majority of the multi-day whale-watching cruises to Baja California and the Sea of Cortez. In the 80- to 105-foot range, most are wide, roomy, well-appointed vessels with carpets, air-conditioning, and a large comfortable central salon. Sturdy and seaworthy, they are designed for extended fishing trips far offshore. Cabins tend to be small, and bathrooms and showers are usually shared. Operators generally take 16 to 32 passengers on extended trips.

Sight-Seeing Cruise Boats

Designed expressly for sight-seeing, these vessels usually have several viewing decks and large cabins with big windows. In addition to being more comfortable than charter fishing boats, they tend to be faster. A few of those listed are large, modern high-speed catamarans. In Alaska the operators of this type of vessel often include elaborate buffet meals. Some of the bigger boats in southern California are large enough to accommodate several hundred passengers.

Sailing Yachts and Luxury Yachts

Sailing silently on the wind alongside whales is a unique experience, and sailing captains claim that the whales appreciate the absence of motors. True or not, these boats do combine two wonderful experiences, sailing and whale watching. A few operators offer short sailboat trips lasting from a few hours up to a day.

On the upscale end of whale-watching trips are the multi-day cruises on sailing yachts and luxury motor yachts. Just you and a handful of other guests aboard a luxury yacht, cruising isolated and beautiful waterways in the Pacific Northwest and dining on gourmet meals prepared from fish and seafood caught hours earlier by the crew. While these trips are more expensive than most of the others in this book, when compared on a daily cost basis to a standard resort hotel they offer a good value for an exceptional experience.

Large Expedition Cruise Vessels

Established companies in the nature and adventure travel business operate these vessels. Passengers sleep in private staterooms, eat in the ship's dining room, and generally enjoy all the amenities of a luxury liner. The differences are that these boats are on a smaller scale, with room for anywhere from a few dozen to a couple hundred passengers, and the cruises are dedicated to viewing marine wildlife and cultural sites. All are accompanied by professional naturalists, often of international repute. Zodiacs take passengers closer to wildlife or to isolated onshore locations. These companies provide a high-quality educational travel experience. Trips generally last from one to two weeks.

Cruise Liners

Dozens of full-size cruise ships ply the waters of the Pacific Northwest, from Seattle up to Alaska, and many of their brochures advertise whale watching as an available activity. When the ships make their scheduled stops in southeast Alaska, often in Sitka, those passengers who wish can board one of the local charter boats, some of which are listed in this book, for a few hours of whale watching.

Ferries

Automobile and passenger ferries run throughout the Pacific Northwest, from Seattle to Alaska, and the companies operating them often advertise whale watching as part of the experience. Yes, you may see whales from a ferry, which would be a very nice bonus to the ride. But don't count on it. If you are going to the Northwest and seeing whales is one of your goals, book a real whale-watching trip.

Would You Like to Make a Reservation?

Of course you would. Always call or write in advance for information and reservations. This could be months ahead for an extended cruise or just hours before a short local trip. But always call. Every effort has been made to ensure that the information in this book is accurate and up to date, but things change. So call and confirm times, prices, policies regarding children, and trip availability; also ask for clear directions to the dock and for parking information. Arrive at least a half-hour before scheduled departure—there is nothing more disappointing than sprinting for the dock to find your boat backing away and turning out to sea.

If you call to arrange a trip for the same or next day, ask about sea and weather conditions and if whales are being sighted in the area. You are almost certain to see whales in some situations, including the gray whale migration, orca watching in the San Juan Islands, or humpback watching in southeast Alaska. Captains maintain radio contact with fishing boats and with each other to track whales, and a number of southern California operators cooperatively employ a spotter plane to find the animals. Some operators guarantee you'll see whales—or at least dolphins—and offer a "whale check" good for a free trip some other time if you don't. Ask about guarantees when you call.

Does Whale Watching Bother the Whales?"

A fair question. Scientists and whale experts almost unanimously say no, as long as it is done responsibly. These people argue that the great majority of commercial whale-watching operators are careful to follow the National Marine Fisheries Services whale-watching guidelines. (If they didn't, their own passengers would probably report them.) More often than not, private boaters are the ones who harass whales, usually due to a lack of knowledge, and cause them to modify their behavior. The official whale-watching guidelines from the National Marine Fisheries Service are as follows:

- Vessels should not be operated at speeds faster than a whale or group of whales while paralleling them within 100 yards.
- Vessels should be operated at a constant speed while paralleling or following whales within 100 yards.

• Vessels should do nothing to cause the whale to change directions.

• Aircraft should not fly lower than 1,000 feet while within a horizontal distance of 100 yards from a whale.

Generally, the whale's usual behavior should not be interrupted. Such an annoyance may cause the whale to change direction rapidly, to swim faster, or to swim in an erratic pattern. Vessels should not approach whales directly from the front or chase them from directly behind. To hinder a whale's normal activities constitutes harassment and is against the law.

If you see a boat violating these guidelines, take down its name and registration number, and report it to the Coast Guard when you return to shore. Better yet, videotape it.

About Seasickness

If you have never experienced seasickness, you are a lucky individual. That or you have never been out whale watching in the Gulf of the Farallons in a big swell. Seasickness strikes when the eyes and inner ear get into a dispute and the brain can't figure out which way you're traveling. For some reason, your stomach pays the price. If you're concerned about seasickness, consider the following advice.

First, if you haven't had experience on the ocean and don't know if you're prone to seasickness, or you don't know if anyone in your family gets seasick, try taking a short cruise. There are few things as hellish as finding yourself seasick half an hour into an all-day ocean trip. Also, be aware that the larger the boat, the less it rocks; if given the choice, pick an 85-foot boat over a 32-foot boat. If you tend to get seasick and nothing can remedy it, don't give up on whale watching. Much of the best whale watching on the West Coast takes place in calm protected waters, such as in the San Juan Islands near Seattle, the Johnstone Strait region of Vancouver Island, and the Inside Passage of Southeast Alaska.

A number of over-the-counter medicines help prevent motion sickness, including Dramamine, the old standby, and Bonine and Marazine. Ask your pharmacist for advice and about side effects, which usually include drowsiness. These products will do the trick for many people; just remember to follow the instructions and take them at least half an hour before going aboard.

Scopolamine patches, sold under the trade name Transderm-V, are small, round disks that you wear like a Band-Aid on the hairless skin behind and below your ear. This is pretty powerful stuff. They work for the majority of people who aren't helped by tablets, and are available only with a prescription. The patch should be applied

12 hours before the trip begins and can be worn for up to three days. (They even stay on in the shower.) Side effects include "dry mouth" and minor drowsiness.

Some people swear by a simple mechanical device that's sold in many large drugstores. This elastic wristband holds a small metal button in place over an acupuncture pressure point, relieving nausea. The instructions tell you how to find the pressure point on your wrist, and the elastic maintains a constant pressure. Aside from the marks left on your skin temporarily, there are no side effects.

Whether or not you choose one of these remedies, be sure to take the following basic precautions:

• Always start your medication ahead of time, per instructions. If you're fumbling with the scopolamine patch while on the way to the dock or taking your pills as the boat pulls away, the medicine won't help.

• Get a good night's sleep, arrive fresh, and don't show up with a hangover unless you are a true masochist.

• Eat lightly before the trip. Avoid greasy, heavy foods and alcohol before and during the voyage.

• During the trip, munch steadily on plain crackers or bread, and keep sipping a carbonated beverage. Ginger ale is the best.

• Pick a spot near the center of the boat to minimize movement, stay outside in the fresh air if possible, keep your eyes on the horizon, and bend with the waves, as if you were surfing the boat.

• Activity can distract your mind from the nausea, so keep busy. Talk to people, listen to the naturalist's lecture, walk around, and scan the horizon.

• Stay warm, but don't remain inside.

• Avoid those who have lost the battle and are hanging over the rail.

• If you succumb, head for the downwind rail. On a boat that has several decks, it's the expected courtesy to use the lowest deck. Don't feel defeated: Admiral Nelson got seasick.

The good news is that whales are the best cure for seasickness. This author can attest that as soon as spouts are sighted and the watching begins, the seasickness just disappears.

What to Wear/What to Bring

You can ruin your whale-watching trip by not dressing warmly enough. Be prepared for waves and weather. Ask about weather conditions when you call for reservations. Even when it's sunny and warm at the harbor, offshore it can be 20 degrees colder and blowing up a gale. Put on several layers of clothing, including a waterproof outer layer. Don't forget a hat, scarf, and gloves; they may mean the difference between a comfortable trip and a cold, miserable one. Wear long pants, socks, and rubber-soled shoes or sneakers (deck-soled rubber boots are perfect for smaller boats in wet conditions). And make sure your kids do the same, particularly teenagers, who often end up huddled miserably in the cabin wearing shorts, sandals, and T-shirts.

After warm clothing, the two essentials are sunscreen and sunglasses (preferably polarized). Use the sunscreen even on overcast days; several hours on the water can leave you fried. Binoculars are very important. If you don't have a pair, borrow one, or use your first whale-watching trip as an excuse to treat yourself. Prices keep going down, and perfectly acceptable rubberized models are available for $50 at discount stores.

Wear a "keeper strap" around your neck for all sunglasses, cameras, binoculars, etc. Attach one to your hat if possible. At least one hat is blown into the water on most whale-watching cruises.

Photographic Equipment

Most people bring cameras and camcorders, and we won't discourage you from doing the same. But be aware that even the pros find it difficult to take good photos of whales on the open ocean. The boat is usually moving too much to use a telephoto lens, and the whales are usually far enough away that a normal or wide-angle lens captures only a dark speck in a big seascape. Add to that the number of people on the rail trying to see and shoot all at once and you get some idea of the difficulties you face. You might do just as well with a compact mini-zoom that fits in your pocket as you would with the best SLR and all its lenses. Whichever you choose, bring high-speed film to compensate for the motion of the boat and the subjects. Also be sure to keep your expensive gear protected from the salt spray, which can destroy it. And don't get so caught up in trying to frame the perfect photo that you miss the live action. If you leave the equipment behind, you can take in the whole scene with all your senses. Your mind will record much better images than your camera ever could.

The situation is completely different if you are taking an extended cruise on a larger boat or booking a private charter with just a few people, particularly on the placid inside waters of the Northwest. Then you can feel comfortable bringing the works. You may be able to set up a tripod on deck and get some excellent telephoto shots. Still, remember to give yourself plenty of time to see the whales through your own eyes.

Whale Behavior—What to Look For

Here are some of the typical whale behaviors you may encounter.

Spouting: The spout is the whale's explosive exhalation of breath through the blowholes upon surfacing from a dive. The moisture-laden air vaporizes into a steamy column. Each of the great whales has its own signature spout in terms of size and shape.

Breaching: Breaching is when a whale leaps partially or entirely out of the water and then slams back into the sea with a huge splash, a spectacular display for which there is no single accepted explanation among cetologists. Possibilities include courtship display, warnings to other whales, shaking off parasites, and just plain having fun.

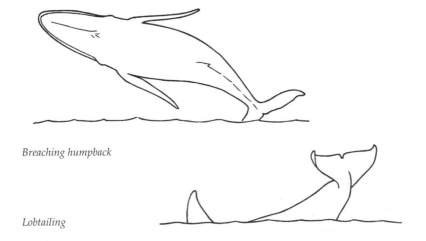

Breaching humpback

Lobtailing

Diving: Each species has a preferred method of diving. Some, like the blue whale, barely flex their bodies, slipping beneath the waves with only the slightest raising of tail flukes above the surface. Others, like grays and humpbacks, bend their backs and raise their flukes high in the air before heading down for a dive.

Spyhopping: Some species, including humpbacks and grays, will thrust their heads straight up until their eyes clear the surface, basically standing on their tails, and remain there while looking around. Sometimes they rotate slowly to get a full 360 degree view. One theory is that gray whales do this to pick up landmarks by which to navigate in their journeys up and down the coast.

Spyhopping orca

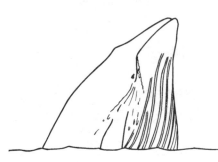

Thrust feeding humpback

Lobtailing: Some whales will, with their heads submerged, raise their tails out of the water and slap them down with a huge splash and loud report. This may be communication, an aggression display toward other whales, or just that old exuberance.

How to Watch Seals, Sea Lions, and Sea Otters

Because of their close ties to land, seals, sea lions, and sea otters present excellent opportunities for viewing, allowing people to spend many hours observing their fascinating behavior. Many inhabit coastal waters, and all must return to land regularly, bringing them within range of landlubbing and seafaring marine-life enthusiasts alike. As you drive along the Coast Highway of California, Oregon, and Washington, or hike along coastal paths, be on the lookout for heads bobbing in the surf offshore (they could be seals, sea lions, or sea otters) and smooth, sleek bodies draped over rocks, basking in the sun, or playing tag.

Always have your binoculars handy, as opportunities for witnessing natural behaviors up close can present themselves at any moment. To enjoy the quiet and solitude of the more out-of-the-way spots, arm yourself with a good coastal access guide and check local tide tables, available at bait and tackle shops.

Low tide is the best time to find seals. But don't let your explorations carry you onto pocket beaches when the tide is coming in. Be aware that as you are watching seals they may be watching you, and take care not to disturb them. If you venture out with a little patience and a lot of respect for these unique creatures, seal watching can become the habit of a lifetime.

These sleek animals can be encountered anywhere along thousands of miles of coastline—on offshore rocks, cobbled or sandy beaches, reefs and ledges, and in lagoons and estuaries—even inland, miles upriver. You may track them down in a serene cove or find them in the hurly-burly settings of Monterey's Fisherman's Wharf, San Francisco's Pier 39, or Seattle's bustling Ballard Shipping Locks.

Sea otters share many habitats with seals and sea lions. The southern sea otter population is concentrated in California's Monterey Bay and the Channel Islands. The northern population thrives in Alaskan waters.

If you're planning to go pinniped/sea otter watching in restricted-access areas such as Año Nuevo or the Channel Islands, it's best to call ahead, because hours vary seasonally and reservations may be required. You should inquire as to whether rangers or volunteers will be presenting special lectures. Check the "Resources" section at the end of chapters 4 through 9 for contact information.

If you are considering taking a boat tour, ask the operator what the wildlife emphasis is and what expectations they have for seeing marine mammals other than whales.

Whale Watching by the Month

The following is a month-by-month breakdown of the best in West Coast whale watching. While there is no guarantee the whales will follow this schedule, experience in recent years indicates your chances of seeing them are pretty good. References to the beginning and end of a particular season are based more on the availability of scheduled whale-watching tours than on the presence of whales. In most areas, boats are available for charter at any time, and in a number of places some of the best whale watching takes place on a private boat just after the main visitor season ends.

CALENDAR

JAN
Alaska: For winter-hardy watchers, humpbacks in Sitka.
Oregon: Southbound gray whale migration in full swing.
California: Southbound gray whale migration in full swing.
Baja California: Cruises to gray whale lagoons, offshore islands, and the Sea of Cortez.

FEB
Oregon: Gray whale migration.
California: Gray whale migration.
Baja California: Cruises to gray whale lagoons, offshore islands, and the Sea of Cortez.

MAR
British Columbia: Tofino gray whale migration.
Washington: Northbound gray whale migration, Pacific Coast.
Oregon: Gray whale migration.
California: Gray whale migration. Mendocino and Fort Bragg whale festivals.
Baja California: Cruises to gray whale lagoons, offshore islands, and the Sea of Cortez.

APR
British Columbia: Tofino gray whale migration.
Washington: Northbound gray whale migration, Pacific Coast.
Oregon: Gray whale migration.
California: Gray whale migration.
Baja California: Last month of season for cruises to gray whale lagoons, offshore islands, and the Sea of Cortez.

MAY
Alaska: Season just opening up in southeast Alaska. Humpbacks and other species.
British Columbia: End of northbound gray whale migration; Tofino resident grays.
Washington: Orca season begins in the San Juan Islands and Puget Sound. End of northbound gray whale migration on Pacific Coast.
Oregon: End of gray whale migration; beginning of summer resident grays.
California: End of gray whale migration.

JUN
Alaska: Season in full swing through September. Humpbacks and other species; cruises.
British Columbia: Johnstone Strait orcas. Tofino resident grays.
Washington: Puget Sound orcas.
Oregon: Resident grays.
California: Humpbacks and blue whales at the Farallon Islands, Channel Islands, and offshore Monterey Bay.

CALENDAR

JUL

Alaska: Fin and sei whales near Kodiak. Orcas at Stikine River delta near Petersburg. Humpbacks and other species.
British Columbia: Johnstone Strait orcas. Tofino resident grays. Queen Charlotte Islands species.
Washington: Puget Sound orcas.
Oregon: Resident grays.
California: Humpbacks and blue whales at the Farallon Islands, Channel Islands, and offshore Monterey Bay.

AUG

Alaska: Humpbacks and other species in most locations.
British Columbia: Johnstone Strait orcas. Possible blue whales off Queen Charlotte Islands. Tofino resident grays.
Washington: Puget Sound orcas.
Oregon: Resident grays.
California: Humpbacks and blue whales at the Farallon Islands, Channel Islands, and offshore Monterey Bay.

SEP

Alaska: End of season for most operators.
British Columbia: Johnstone Strait orcas. Tofino resident grays.
Washington: Puget Sound orcas.
Oregon: Resident grays.
California: Humpbacks and blue whales at the Farallon Islands, Channel Islands, and offshore Monterey Bay.

OCT

Alaska: Humpbacks near Sitka.
British Columbia: End of Johnstone Strait orca season. Last month for Tofino's resident grays.
Washington: End of orca season in Puget Sound for most operators.
Oregon: Resident grays.
California: Humpbacks and blue whales at the Farallon Islands, Channel Islands, and offshore Monterey Bay.

NOV

Alaska: Best time to see Kodiak humpbacks, but watch out for Gulf of Alaska storms.
Oregon: Beginning of southbound gray whale migration.
California: Humpbacks and blue whales at the Farallon Islands, Channel Islands, and offshore Monterey Bay.

DEC

Alaska: Good humpback viewing near Sitka, for winter-hardy watchers.
Oregon: Beginning of southbound gray whale migration.
California: Southbound gray whale migration. Last of humpbacks and blues.
Baja California: First cruises of season to gray whale lagoons, offshore islands, and the Sea of Cortez.

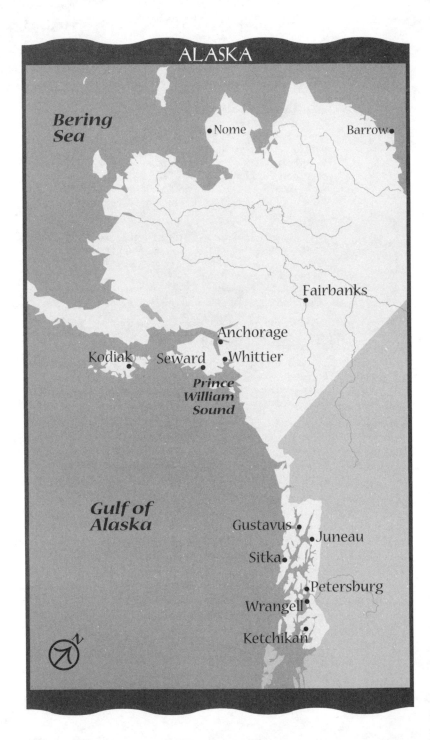

4

ALASKA

The "Great State" of Alaska is one of the best places in the world for whale watching. Many whales migrate to Alaska's nutrient-rich seas to spend their summers with a wide array of resident marine mammals in one of the most beautiful and abundant ecosystems on earth. This book covers the southern and southeastern Alaskan coast, including Kodiak Island, the westernmost point with regular whale-watching operations.

Alaska's whale-watching opportunities run the gamut from half-day tours to two-week adventure cruises, and you can choose between roughing it in a kayak or sailing on an ultraluxurious private yacht. Services tend to be more expensive here than elsewhere along the West Coast: adult fares for the least expensive half-day tours range from $60 to $90.

Those of us who are prone to seasickness will enjoy the fact that much of Alaska's whale watching takes place in the usually placid waters of the Inside Passage, which doesn't experience the massive swells of the Gulf of Alaska.

Although the majority of Alaska's visitors come between June and September, whale watching is available throughout most of the year. In fact, locals tout early winter as a prime time to see whales. Then, the summer crowds are gone and you can negotiate some good deals. Humpbacks are resident all winter, which is surprisingly mild on Alaska's southeast coast; there's little snowfall and on most days the temperature is above freezing. (One drawback: you might have to wait for a Gulf storm to clear before your boat can depart.) The folks in Sitka say they have the best location for winter whale watching, and they invite you to come when the whales are close to shore and the tourists are far away.

Kodiak Island

The Russian explorer Stephan Glutov discovered Kodiak Island in 1763. It was settled in 1784 by his countryman Alexander Baranov, a fur trader in search of sea otter pelts. Baranov established the town of Kodiak in 1792 as the capital of Russia's North American colonies. Onion-domed Orthodox churches are standing reminders of the town's Russian roots.

Today Kodiak is the commercial center of the Gulf of Alaska's incredibly rich fisheries industry. There is air service between Kodiak and Anchorage and a weekly ferry from the mainland.

Gray whales pass Kodiak Island in the spring on their northward migration, and their numbers are at their peak from late March to mid-April. Humpbacks, whose density varies seasonally, can be seen every month, with the greatest activity taking place in November, when up to several hundred may be in the area at one time. Pods of orcas that are transient, rather than resident, are spotted regularly, with the highest concentration usually in August. Fin and sei whales are often spotted in July, while minkes are in the area year-round.

Dall's and harbor porpoises are fairly common, as are Steller's sea lions and harbor seals. Pacific white-sided dolphins are occasionally sighted.

Over the years the local sea otter population has grown into the thousands, and they can be viewed easily from accessible shore points in the fall and winter, when they move from exposed and isolated points and capes into more protected bays and inlets.

In addition to having major seabird rookeries and bald eagle nesting sites, Kodiak Island boasts the Kodiak brown bear, the world's largest terrestrial carnivore.

Several onshore whale-viewing sites are accessible by car from Kodiak. At Fort Abercrombie State Park you can spot gray whales in the spring and humpbacks in the summer. Narrow Cape is a good place to catch the spring migration of gray whales, as is Cape Chiniak.

Prince William Sound

Prince William Sound is one of the richest fishing grounds and wildlife areas in the world. In 1989 it suffered what some consider to be the greatest environmental disaster in history, when the Exxon *Valdez* oil tanker ran aground on Bligh Reef and spilled 11 million gallons of oil into the pristine waters of the Sound. The incompetent emergency response by the oil companies compounded the tragedy and permitted the spill to spread, eventually fouling over 1,200 miles of coastline and reaching as far as Kodiak Island.

Despite the heroic efforts of volunteers to rescue and rehabilitate as many oil-drenched animals as possible, an estimated two to three thousand sea otters died, in addition to hundreds of thousands of seabirds. This ecological disaster notwithstanding, the Sound is spectacular, with little noticeable damage—on the surface. Although the full impact may not be known for decades, this remains a major habitat for sea otters, Steller's and California sea lions, harbor seals, birds, and other wildlife. Humpback whales and orcas are occasionally spotted, but this is not one of the best whale-watching areas.

Resurrection Bay

Resurrection Bay is surrounded by mountains and ice fields. Wildlife cruises out of Seward take in Resurrection Bay and Kenai Fjords National Park; 580,000 acres of the coastal Kenai Mountain range; and Harding Ice Field, one of the largest in the United States.

Gray whales are seen during their April return migration. Humpbacks, fins, and orcas are spotted with varying frequency. In addition to Dall's and harbor porpoises, Steller's and California sea lions, harbor seals, and sea otters, there are marine birds and bald eagles.

Glacier Bay

Only two hundred years ago, Glacier Bay was under five thousand feet of ice. Sixteen tidewater glaciers calve icebergs into the 60-mile-long bay, which is dominated by 15,320-foot Mount Fairweather. Glacier Bay National Park is one of Alaska's prime attractions and is usually home to humpback, orca, and minke whales. Unfortunately, extremely restrictive regulations are imposed on boats licensed to take people into the bay, making this a poor place to watch whales. It was believed that the large number of cruise ships and smaller private craft that crowded into the bay in the early 1970s to watch whales drove away a resident population of humpbacks. Now boats cannot approach whales, slow down, or in any way alter their course if whales are sighted, and must remain so far away that it's hard to see the animals.

Fortunately, just outside the entrance to Glacier Bay, off Point Adolphus and in nearby Icy Strait, large resident populations of humpback whales provide the best whale watching in southeast Alaska. Minkes and orcas are spotted less frequently, as are harbor porpoises and the occasional Dall's porpoise. There are Steller's sea lions and harbor seals. Sea otters have been recolonizing the area in recent years. Gustavus, near the national park headquarters, is home to several whale-watching operations. Glacier Bay Lodge,

49

within the park, and a number of local inns and bed-and-breakfasts offer package deals on lodging and whale-watching treks.

INSIDE PASSAGE

Alaska's southeast panhandle is bordered by the famed Inside Passage, a channel containing hundreds of islands, glaciers, mountainous fjords, and incomparable scenery and wildlife. The sea penetrates into the deep fjords and myriad islands, creating strong currents and great tidal changes that boost productivity in the nearshore waters—a fact not lost on the marine mammal community. Much of the area is part of the Tongass National Forest, at 17 million acres the largest of the national forests. Visitor services and accommodations are well developed in this region, which is home to over a score of established whale-watching operators. The ferries of Alaska's Marine Highway system ply the Inside Passage of the southeast panhandle and offer some opportunities to see whales.

Sitka

The town of Sitka is steeped in several hundred years of Alaskan history and has been the site of some of the state's most important events. Home for centuries to the Kiskadi clan of the Tlingit people, the seafront village of Shee Atika was changed forever in 1799 by the arrival of Russian fur traders. Relations between the natives and the newcomers started off bad and quickly grew worse, culminating in the Tlingit attack of 1802 on the Russian outpost near the village. The Russians returned in force two years later and after a weeklong siege, took back the village. Alexander Baranov, manager of the Russian-American Company and founder of Kodiak, moved his colony's capital from Kodiak to Sitka and made the town the center of Russian Alaska's commerce and culture. The Tlingit moved back in 1821, and many current residents are Native Americans. There is much evidence of both cultures, including Saint Michael's Russian Orthodox Cathedral; the Russian Bishop's House, built in 1842; the Sheldon Jackson Museum of native culture; and the Southeast Alaska Indian Cultural Center.

Sitka is a major draw for those who visit southeast Alaska during the summer, and most cruise lines that operate in the state stop here. It can get busy in the high season (June through August). Alaska Airlines services Sitka year-round, and offers nonstop flights from Seattle.

Sitka offers excellent and accessible whale and marine mammal watching year-round. Sitka Sound is home to a stable humpback whale population, and animals are in the area all year. October to

January finds the greatest concentration closest to town, with the most spectacular behaviors and vocalizations. Males may be practicing their famous mating songs, perhaps tuning up for the breeding season in the waters of Hawaii and Mexico. Gray whales pass by on their northbound migration in April. Transient pods of orcas are spotted here on an irregular basis most of the year. Minke whales are also seen occasionally.

Smaller cetacean species commonly spotted are harbor and Dall's porpoises and, in recent years farther offshore in the Gulf of Alaska, Pacific white-sided dolphins. Steller's sea lions and harbor seals are common to the area, with occasional sightings of Northern fur seals. Another major attraction near Sitka is the large resident population of sea otters, which can be observed on most wildlife cruises.

There is an abundance of marine bird life in the region. Fifteen miles from Sitka, Saint Lazaria Wildlife Refuge is a major seabird rookery, home to hundreds of thousands of roosting tufted puffins, murres, petrels, rhinoceros auklets, and other species.

Worth a visit in Sitka is the Alaska Raptor Rehabilitation Center, a nonprofit private organization that rehabilitates injured birds of prey from around the state and, when possible, returns them to the wild. (For information, contact: ARRC, Box 2984, Sitka, AK 99835; 907/747–8662.)

Frederick Sound

Humpback whales are found year-round in Frederick Sound, with June to October the months of greatest numbers and activity. Transient orca pods are frequently seen in the area, and minke whales are occasionally spotted. Dall's and harbor porpoises are common. Pacific white-sided dolphins have been spotted more frequently in recent years, and groups of thousands have been seen near Wrangell.

Steller's sea lion rookeries are found in Frederick Sound as well as the Stikine River, which also has a large harbor seal rookery. June is pupping season, and when the pups are weaned, approximately six weeks later, orcas arrive to feed on both salmon and the young seals. Sea otters are slowly recolonizing their former range and are sometimes seen.

Petersburg has been a Norwegian outpost since it was established in 1897 as a sawmill and salmon cannery by founder Peter Buschmann. Still an active shrimping, fishing, and logging center, Petersburg is located just off Frederick Sound and within a short cruise to Le Conte Bay, Le Conte Glacier, and the Stikine River Delta, all areas of magnificent scenery and abundant wildlife, including marine, avian, and terrestrial animals.

On Easter Sunday, 1994, a pod of orcas chased a pod of Pacific white-sided dolphins into Petersburg Harbor and for 45 minutes pursued the panicked creatures around boats, docks, and pilings. Most of the town's residents came down to watch the spectacle.

Ketchikan

Ketchikan is the southernmost city in Alaska and the wettest city in North America, receiving over 150 inches of rain per year. It's billed as the "Salmon Capital of the World," a claim that might be disputed by many Pacific Northwest communities. Ketchikan also boasts the world's largest collection of totem poles and is the closest town to the Misty Fjords National Monument, an area of beautiful scenery that's rich with wildlife, including whales. The waters right around Ketchikan are not good for whale watching because the closest feeding grounds are too far away for short day trips by boat. Aerial tours and extended cruises are more appropriate.

One hundred miles west of Ketchikan on the outer coast there's a lot of whale activity, and one can spot humpbacks, migrating grays, and orcas.

Regional Extended Tour Operators

Bluewater Adventures

252 East First Street, #3
North Vancouver, BC, V7L 1B3 Canada
604/980–3800

Owner: Randy Burke.
Season: May to October.
Boat: S. V. *Island Roamer,* a 68-foot sailing ketch, 16 passengers.
Times: Five- to 11-day trips throughout the Pacific Northwest, including southeast Alaska, the Queen Charlotte Islands, Vancouver Island, and the San Juan and Gulf islands.
Cost: $875 to $2,500 per person (in U.S. currency).
Departs: Various ports in the Pacific Northwest.
Refreshments: Onboard meals and accommodations included.
Miscellaneous: Over 20 years' experience in wildlife cruises. Zoos, museums, and other organizations often book passage on their cruises for members. Inflatables and kayaks are available. Expert naturalists accompany all trips.

Dolphin Charters

1007 Leneve Place
El Cerrito, CA 94530
510/527–9622

Captain: Ronn Storro-Patterson.
Season: June to September.
Boat: M. V. *Delphinus*, a 50-foot motor yacht designed for natural history cruises, 12 passengers.
Times: Seven- to 12-night natural history expedition cruises in southeastern Alaska and the Inside Passage.
Cost: $1,995 to $3,895 per person.
Departs: Ketchikan, Petersburg, Juneau.
Refreshments: All onboard meals included.
Miscellaneous: Dolphin Charters specializes in natural history cruises and education. Captain Storro-Patterson is a professional biologist and a former university professor. Fare includes one flight on a three-passenger SeaBee seaplane; additional flights are available for a fee.

Glacier Bay Tours and Cruises / Glacier Bay Lodge

520 Pike Street, Suite 1610
Seattle, WA 98101
907/697–2226, 800/451–5952

Season: May to September.
Boats: A fleet of cruise boats and ships, including M. V. *Wilderness Explorer*, a 112-foot mini–cruise ship with 18 cabins, 36 passengers; M. V. *Executive Explorer*, a 100-foot catamaran with 25 staterooms, 49 passengers; M. V. *World Discoverer*, a 285-foot expedition ship with 70 staterooms, 138 passengers; and Holland America Line luxury cruise ships.
Times: From half-day excursions to 17-day cruise/tour packages.
Cost: $89 to over $7,000 per person.
Departs: Most ports in Alaska and the Pacific Northwest.
Miscellaneous: Glacier Bay Tours and Cruises has been providing whale-watching and adventure cruises in Alaska for nearly 30 years. Their entertaining, colorful, and informative brochure offers a bewildering array of tour options, cruises, and packages. Professional naturalists accompany all cruises. Kayaks and Zodiac inflatables are taken on all multi-day trips (except on Holland America).

Nature Expeditions International
474 Willamette Street
P.O. Box 11496
Eugene, OR 97440
503/484–6529, 800/869–0639

Director: Chris Kyle.
Season: June to September.
Boat: M. V. *World Discoverer,* a 285-foot adventure cruising vessel, 135 passengers.
Times: Eight- to 15-day wildlife expeditions and cruises.
Cost: $2,490 to $5,200 per person.
Departs: Homer, Nome, and Prince Rupert, BC.
Refreshments: All meals included.
Miscellaneous: Nature Expeditions has over 20 years of experience in the field of adventure travel. Experienced naturalists and research biologists accompany all expeditions. Boat is equipped with Zodiac inflatables.

Oceanic Society Expeditions
Fort Mason Center, Building E
San Francisco, CA 94123
415/474–3385

Season: July to September.
Boat: S. V. *Island Roamer,* a 68-foot sailing ketch, 16 passengers.
Times: Five- to 12-day cruises.
Cost: $1,250 to $2,990 per person.
Departs: Various regional ports.
Refreshments: All meals included.
Miscellaneous: A major nonprofit cetacean research and education organization, Oceanic Society Expeditions has been offering marine natural history tours for over 20 years. Highly experienced naturalists lead all cruises.

Special Expeditions, Inc.
720 Fifth Avenue
New York, NY 10019
212/765–7740, 800/762–0003

Founder: Sven-Olof Lindblad.
Season: June to August.
Boat: M. V. *Sea Bird* and M. V. *Sea Lion,* 152-foot custom-built coastal cruise ships, 70 passengers each.
Times: Eight- to 12-day cruises through the waters of southeast Alaska.
Cost: $1,990 to $4,880 per person.
Departs: Juneau, Sitka.

Refreshments: All onboard meals included.

Miscellaneous: Special Expeditions has been offering wildlife cruises worldwide since 1979 and is one of the most experienced operators in the field. All cruises are staffed by professional naturalists and research biologists. Zodiacs are used to get closer to wildlife.

Kodiak Island Tour Operators

Eagle Adventures

P.O. Box 2898
Kodiak, AK 99615
907/486–3445

Captain: Larry Shaker.
Season: May to December.
Boat: *Chaik,* a 50-foot custom-built charter boat, 18 passengers.
Times: Full-day trips.
Cost: $135 per person.
Departs: Kodiak Harbor.
Refreshments: Drinks and lunch provided.
Miscellaneous: In operation since 1988. Trips are narrated by an experienced captain.

Kodiak Island Charters

P.O. Box 3750
Kodiak, AK 99615
907/486–5380, 800/575–5380

Captain: Chris Fiala.
Season: March 15 to December.
Boat: *U-Rascal,* a 43-foot charter vessel; six passengers.
Times: Full-day trips by arrangement.
Cost: $175 per person.
Departs: Kodiak Harbor.
Refreshments: Beverages, lunch, and snacks provided.
Miscellaneous: In operation since 1989. Trips are narrated by an experienced captain.

Kodiak Nautical Discoveries

P.O. Box 95
Kodiak, AK 99615
907/486–4971, 206/633–5124

Captain: Dr. Ron Brockman.
Season: June to October; year-round for charters.
Boat: *The Sea Surgeon,* a 42-foot cabin cruiser, six passengers.
Times: Half- and full-day trips; multi-day charters.

Cost: $100 per person half-day; $150 full day; $300 a day per person for multi-day charters.

Departs: Kodiak Harbor, Kiliuda Bay, and other Kodiak locations.

Refreshments: Beverages and snacks on half-day trips; lunch included on full-day trips; all meals and accommodations on multi-day charters.

Miscellaneous: Born and raised on Kodiak Island, Dr. Brockman has a degree in biology, 30 years' experience as a charter captain, and 5 years' experience running his own wildlife trips. Kodiak Nautical Discoveries takes their clients to remote locations to explore for marine wildlife.

Kodiak Western Charters

P.O. Box 4123
Kodiak, AK 99615
907/486–2200

Captain: Eric Stirrup.

Season: April to December.

Boat: *Ten Bears*, a 50-foot motor vessel, 14 passengers on day trips, 6 passengers for charters.

Times: Full-day trips and multi-day live-aboard charters.

Cost: $160 per person for day trips; multi-day by arrangement.

Departs: Near Island, Saint Herman's Boat Harbor.

Refreshments: Drinks and snacks provided on day trips; all meals included on extended charters.

Miscellaneous: Captain Stirrup, a marine biologist and former research biologist, has been chartering on Kodiak Island for over a decade. Hydrophone on board.

Prince William Sound Tour Operators

Major Marine Tours

509 West Third Street
Anchorage, AK 99501
907/274–7300, 800/764–7300

Captain: Chris Overbeck.

Season: Late May to Labor Day.

Boat: M. V. *Emerald Sea*, a 100-foot custom-built coastal sightseeing vessel with two decks, 149 passengers.

Times: Six-hour Prince William Sound and Blackstone Glacier cruise leaves daily at 11:15 A.M.

Cost: $89 per person; half-price for children under 13.

Departs: Whittier.

Refreshments: All-you-can-eat salmon dinner and dessert bar included.

Miscellaneous: In operation out of Whittier since 1990. Cruise is narrated by experienced captain, and the crew is trained to answer questions. Wheelchair accessible.

Phillips Cruises & Tours

509 West Fourth Avenue
Anchorage, AK 99501
907/276–8023, 800/544–0529

Season: May to mid-September.
Boat: M. V. *Klondike Express*, a 102-foot high-speed catamaran, 265 passengers.
Times: Six-hour "26 Glacier Tour" to College and Harriman Fjords daily at 11:15 A.M.
Cost: $119 per person; $49 for children under 12.
Departs: Whittier.
Refreshments: Hot luncheon included.
Miscellaneous: Operating since 1958. Experienced crews narrate trips. Wheelchair accessible.

Resurrection Bay Tour Operators

Kenai Fjords Tours

P.O. Box 1889
Seward, AK 99664
907/224–8068, 800/478–8068

Owner: Tom Tougas.
Season: Late April to September; charters per demand the rest of the year.
Boats: Seven custom-built coastal sight-seeing vessels, 50 to 90 feet, 18 to 149 passengers.
Times: Resurrection Bay tour (four hours) departs daily at 8:30 A.M. and 1 P.M.; Kenai Fjords National Park and Chiswell Islands National Wildlife Refuge tour (six to eight hours) departs daily at 8 A.M., 10 A.M., and 11:30 A.M.; gray whale migration tour (four hours) departs daily at 11:30 A.M. (late April only).
Cost: Resurrection Bay—$59 per person, $25 for children under 12; Kenai Fjords—$99 per person, $46 for children; gray whale migration—$74 per person, $37 for children. Add 5 percent sales tax.
Departs: Seward Small Boat Harbor, The Landing.
Refreshments: Galleys on all boats. Lunch included on Kenai Fjords trip.
Miscellaneous: In operation since 1974. Most of the captains live year-round in Seward, and all are trained naturalists. Wheelchairs are accommodated.

Major Marine Tours

509 West Third Street
Anchorage, AK 99501
907/274–7300, 800/764–7300

Captain: Gary Sommerfeld.
Season: Mid-May to mid-September.
Boat: M. V. *Star of the Northwest,* a 115-foot custom-built coastal sight-seeing vessel with three decks, 220 passengers.
Times: Kenai Fjords and Resurrection Bay tours run daily from 12:30 P.M. to 5 P.M. Starting in early June, there's an additional evening trip from 6 P.M. to 10 P.M.
Cost: $74 per person for day trip; $64 for evening trip; half-price for children under 13. Add 5 percent sales tax.
Departs: Seward.
Refreshments: All-you-can-eat crab and shrimp buffet with dessert bar included.
Miscellaneous: Operating out of Seward since 1988. Cruises are narrated by an experienced captain, and the crew is trained to answer questions. Very accessible to wheelchairs.

Mariah Tours and Charters

3812 Katmai Circle
Anchorage, AK 99517–1024
907/243–1238, 800/270–1236

Owner: John Sheedy.
Season: April 20 to October 1.
Boats: *Misty* and *Mariah,* 45-foot custom-built tour boats, 22 passengers each.
Times: Kenai Fjords Wildlife and Glacier tour runs daily from 8 A.M. to 5 P.M.; Northwestern Experience tour runs daily from 8 A.M. to 5:30 P.M.; Resurrection Bay Wildlife tour runs daily from 1 P.M. to 5 P.M.
Cost: Kenai Fjords—$90 per person, $45 for children under 12; Northwestern Experience—$105 per person, $50 for children; Resurrection Bay—$55 per person, $30 for children.
Departs: Seward Harbor.
Refreshments: Bring your own lunch. Beverages are provided.
Miscellaneous: Fifteen years' experience. Crews narrate. Longer tours include the Chiswell Islands National Wildlife Refuge.

Phillips Cruises & Tours

509 West Fourth Avenue
Anchorage, AK 99501
907/276–8023, 800/544–0529

Season: May 20 to September 10.

Boat: M. V. *Klondike,* a 72-foot high-speed catamaran, 165 passengers.
Times: Six-hour tour departs daily at 11:30 A.M.
Cost: $89 per person; $39 for children under 12.
Departs: Seward Small Boat Harbor.
Refreshments: Hot luncheon included.
Miscellaneous: Operating since 1958. Experienced crews provide narration. Wheelchair accessible.

Glacier Bay Tour Operators

Fairweather Fishing and Guide Service

June to August:
P.O. Box 164
Gustavus, AK 99826
907/697–2335

September to May:
P.O. Box 1335
Homer, AK 99603
907/235–3844

Owner: Wayne Clark.
Season: June to mid-September.
Boat: *Tomten,* a 36-foot cabin cruiser, six passengers.
Times: Half-day and full-day trips daily per demand.
Cost: $90 per person half-day; $160 full day.
Departs: Gustavus.
Refreshments: Coffee and beverages. Lunch served on full-day trips.
Miscellaneous: Skipper Clark is an experienced naturalist.

Glacier Bay Country Inn/Grand Pacific Charters

P.O. Box 5
Gustavus, AK 99826
907/697–2288, 801/673–8480 (off-season)

Owners: Annie and Al Unrein.
Season: Mid-May to mid-September.
Boats: Three Bayliner cabin cruisers, 27 to 32 feet, six passengers.
Times: Half-day trips daily around 7:30 A.M. and 1 P.M. There are also full-day and overnight charters.
Cost: $90 per person half-day; $160 full day.
Departs: Gustavus.
Refreshments: Coffee and beverages.
Miscellaneous: In operation since 1986. Accommodations/whale-watching packages available.

Glacier Bay Tours and Cruises/Glacier Bay Lodge

520 Pike Street, Suite 1610
Seattle, WA 98101
907/697–2226, 800/451–5952

Season: May 12 to September 16.
Boat: M. V. *Captain Conner*, a 65-foot restored classic motor yacht and former prisoner-transfer boat, 39 passengers.
Times: Daily 9:30 A.M. and 1:30 P.M.; tours last three hours.
Cost: $89 per person, includes transportation from lodge or airport.
Departs: Gustavus.
Refreshments: Beverages, snacks, and lunch available.
Miscellaneous: Operates out of the Glacier Bay Lodge in the national park. Twenty years' whale-watching experience. Whale sightings guaranteed or your money back.

Glacier Guides, Inc.

June to August:
P.O. Box 219
Gustavus, AK 99826
907/697–2252

September to May:
P.O. Box 460
Santa Clara, UT 84765
801/628–0973

Owner: Jimmie C. Rosenbruch.
Season: June to August.
Boat: *Alaskan Solitude*, a 72-foot custom-built cruise boat, eight passengers maximum for cruises.
Times: Two- to five-night cruises and day charters.
Cost: $1,150 to $3,750 per person for cruises; $2,650 a day for charters.
Departs: Glacier Bay Park.
Refreshments: All meals provided on long cruises and day charters.
Miscellaneous: Alaska Master Guide Jimmie Rosenbruch has been providing luxury fishing and wildlife cruises in Glacier Bay and southeast Alaska since 1965.

Gustavus Marine Charters

P.O. Box 81
Gustavus, AK 99826
907/697–2233

Owner: Mike Nigro.

Season: May to September.
Boats: Two 42-foot cabin cruisers, six passengers each.
Times: Four-hour cruises daily by arrangement.
Cost: $90 per person.
Departs: Gustavus.
Refreshments: Coffee and beverages.
Miscellaneous: Mike has been taking people out whale watching since 1981.

Sea Quest Expeditions/Zoetic Research

P.O. Box 2424
Friday Harbor, WA 98250
206/378–5767

Contact: Mark Lewis, Expedition Director.
Season: May to June.
Boats: Two-person sea kayaks; each trip limited to 12 guests with 2 or 3 guides.
Times: Seven-day kayaking/camping trips.
Cost: $1,199 per person.
Departs: Gustavus.
Refreshments: Breakfast and dinner included on multi-day trips; bring your own snacks for lunch.
Miscellaneous: Zoetic Research is a nonprofit environmental research and education organization. Research biologists accompany every trip. No previous kayaking experience is necessary, but you must be physically fit.

Spirit Walker Expeditions

P.O. Box 240
Gustavus, AK 99826
907/697–2266, 800/529–2537

Contact: Nate Borson, President.
Season: May to September.
Boats: Two-person sea kayaks; each trip limited to 10 guests and 2 guides.
Times: Two- to six-night custom kayaking/camping trips.
Cost: $660 per person for two nights; $1,849 for six nights.
Departs: Gustavus.
Refreshments: All meals included.
Miscellaneous: Offering kayaking/camping trips to Point Adolphus since 1988. All equipment is provided, including sleeping bags, outer gear, and boots. Average of four kayakers and one guide per trip.

INSIDE PASSAGE TOUR OPERATORS

Sitka Tour Operators

Alaskan Waters Unlimited

P.O. Box 6112
Sitka, AK 99835
907/747–5777

Captain: Barbara Bingham.
Season: March to December.
Boat: *Ravensfire,* a 65-foot motor vessel, 45 passengers for day trips, sleeps 18 for charters.
Times: Half- and full-day cruises and multi-day live-aboard research and instruction charters.
Cost: $80 per person half-day; $175 full-day; half-price for children under 13; $300 a day for multi-day trips.
Departs: Sitka.
Refreshments: Beverages on all trips. Lunch provided on full-day cruises. All meals provided on multi-day trips.
Miscellaneous: Bingham has over 10 years' experience skippering wildlife cruises around Sitka. She narrates day trips, and professional instructors accompany multi-day trips. Wheelchair accessible.

Bayside Charters

1601 Sawmill Creek Boulevard
Sitka, AK 99835
907/747–7495

Captain: Bert Stromquist.
Season: May to September.
Boat: *Bluewater,* a 28-foot cabin cruiser, six passengers.
Times: Half- and full-day tours; multi-day trips by request.
Cost: $80 per person half-day; $160 full day.
Departs: Crescent Harbor, Sitka.
Refreshments: Beverages and snacks on half-day trips; lunch provided on full-day trips.
Miscellaneous: Captain Stromquist has a degree in marine biology and has been leading wildlife-viewing charters since 1986.

Sea Otter and Wildlife Quest

P.O. Box 1049
Sitka, AK 99835
907/747–8100

Owners: The Allen family.
Season: May 15 to early September.
Boats: Four 65-foot high-speed custom-built sight-seeing vessels, 49 passengers each.
Times: Three-and-a-half-hour tours on Sunday, Wednesday, and Friday at 2 P.M.
Cost: $80 per person; $40 for children under 13.
Departs: Crescent Harbor.
Refreshments: Beverages and snacks included.
Miscellaneous: The Allen family has been running wildlife tours in the Sitka area for over 20 years. They service the cruise ships that call at Sitka. Naturalists accompany all tours.

Sea Trek

600 Lake Street
Sitka, AK 99835
907/747–8295, 800/747–8295

Captain: Ken Nelson.
Season: May to September.
Boat: *Trekker*, a speedy 25-foot cabin cruiser, six passengers (four preferred).
Times: Custom tours by reservation.
Cost: $75 per person half-day; $135 full day (prices for four to six people).
Departs: Crescent Harbor, Sitka.
Refreshments: Beverages and snacks provided; lunch also on full-day trips.
Miscellaneous: Nelson left commercial fishing in 1994 to provide custom wildlife and fishing charters.

Sitka's Secrets

500 Lincoln Street, #641
Sitka, AK 99835
907/747–5089

Captain: Kent Hall.
Season: April to September.
Boat: *Sitka Secret*, a 26-foot charter boat, six passengers.
Times: Half-day tours by arrangement.
Cost: $80 per person.
Departs: Crescent Harbor, Sitka.
Refreshments: Beverages provided.

Miscellaneous: A husband-wife team with professional degrees in zoology and wildlife management and decades of experience as field biologists, the Halls have been offering tours since 1986.

Steller Charters

2810 Sawmill Creek Boulevard
Sitka, AK 99835
907/747–6157

Captain: Bill Foster.
Season: Year-round.
Boat: *Steller J*, a 28-foot cabin cruiser, six passengers.
Times: Half-day and full-day trips.
Cost: $300 per boat half-day; $400 full day.
Departs: Crescent Harbor, Sitka.
Refreshments: Beverages provided.
Miscellaneous: One of the most experienced naturalist captains in the area, Bill Foster taught biology and science for 30 years and has been running wildlife trips out of Sitka for more than 10 years. Hydrophones are available.

Frederick Sound Tour Operators

Alaskan Scenic Waterways

P.O. Box 943
114 Harbor Way
Petersburg, AK 99833
907/772–3777, 800/279–1176

Captain: Ron Compton.
Season: April to mid-September.
Boats: Three jet boats, the largest a 23-foot heated cabin cruiser capable of shallow-river transit, six passengers each.
Times: Day trips and two- to five-night camping trips by reservation.
Cost: $90 to $140 per person for day trips; $250 a night, all-inclusive, for camping trips.
Departs: Will pick up clients in Wrangell or Petersburg.
Refreshments: All meals included on multi-day trips.
Miscellaneous: Wildlife viewing and photography trips to La Conte Glacier Bay and the Stikine River, where harbor seal and Steller's sea lion rookeries are closely observed. Visitors stay in heated-wall tents. In operation since 1989.

Alaskan Star Charters

P.O. Box 2027
Wrangell, AK 99929
907/874–3084, 918/583–7111

Captain: Ken Wyrick.
Season: May to September.
Boat: *Star Queen,* a 60-foot luxury motor yacht, six passengers.
Times: Five-day cruises, longer by arrangement.
Cost: $2,275 per person for five-day trips.
Departs: Wrangell or Petersburg.
Refreshments: All meals included.
Miscellaneous: Over 10 years' experience.

Alaska Passages

P.O. Box 213
Petersburg, AK 99833
907/772–3967

Captain: Scott Hursey.
Season: April to September.
Boat: M. V. *Heron,* a 65-foot classic wooden motor yacht, four to six passengers.
Times: Six- to 10-day live-aboard cruises.
Cost: $1,695 per person for the first four passengers (fifth and sixth pay half-price) on 6-day trips; $2,495 per person for the first four passengers (fifth and sixth pay half-price) on 10-day trips.
Departs: Petersburg or any port in southeast Alaska.
Refreshments: All meals provided.
Miscellaneous: Scott and Julie Hursey have offered custom-designed sight-seeing cruises in southeast Alaska since 1989. Scott was a commercial fisherman for 22 years before that. Sea kayaks and hydrophone are available.

Sights Southeast

P.O. Box 787
Petersburg, AK 99833
907/772–4503

Captain: Steve Berry.
Season: Late June to September.
Boat: *Eclipse,* a 28-foot cabin cruiser, six passengers.
Times: Six-hour trips depart daily at 6 A.M. and 1 P.M.
Cost: $135 per person.
Departs: Petersburg Harbor.
Refreshments: Beverages and snacks.

Miscellaneous: Steve Berry, the highly knowledgeable captain, has over 20 years' experience with wildlife tours.

Tongass Kayaks

P.O. Box 787
Petersburg, AK 99833
907/772–4600

Captain: Scott Roberge.
Season: Late June to early September.
Boats: Two-person kayaks.
Times: Two-, three-, and six-night kayaking/camping tours in the Frederick Sound/Le Conte Glacier Bay/Stikine River area.
Cost: $395 per person for two nights; $495 per person for three nights; $1,049 per person for six nights.
Departs: Petersburg.
Refreshments: All meals provided.
Miscellaneous: Over 10 years' experience. Roberge works with Steve Berry of Sights Southeast to offer kayaking with humpback whales.

Ketchikan Tour Operators

Alaska Cruises

P.O. Box 7814
Ketchikan, AK 99901
907/225–6044

Owner: Dale Pihlman.
Season: June 1 to September 3.
Boat: *Crystal Fjord,* a 65-foot custom-built sight-seeing vessel, 28 passengers.
Times: Full-day Misty Fjords National Park cruises leave Monday, Wednesday, Thursday, and Sunday at 8 A.M. and return late; cruise/fly-back packages are available; custom whale-watching charters available throughout southeast Alaska.
Cost: $140 per person, $110 for children 2 to 11, free for children under 2; full-day cruise/fly back—$185 per person, $150 for children 2 to 11, free for children under 2.
Departs: Ketchikan Harbor.
Refreshments: Continental breakfast, seafood chowder lunch, and deli dinner included.
Miscellaneous: Dale Pihlman is a marine biologist/naturalist. Other captains are former U.S. Forest Service naturalists. Fifteen years' experience.

Island Wings Air Service

P.O. Box 7432
Ketchikan, AK 99901
907/225–2444

Owner: Michelle Masden.
Season: Late March to September.
Plane: Cessna 185 single-engine floatplane, three passengers.
Times: Three- to four-hour trips (about two to three hours flight time and one hour floating with whales) by arrangement.
Cost: $240 per air hour per plane.
Departs: Ketchikan Airport.
Refreshments: Picnic lunch provided.
Miscellaneous: Masden, a pilot and commercial fisher, has been taking people on air/float whale-watching trips since 1991. When humpbacks are sighted she puts down nearby, cuts the engine, climbs out on the pontoons with her passengers, and lets the plane drift with the whales.

Misty Fjords Air & Outfitting

1285 Tongass Avenue
Ketchikan, AK 99901
907/225–5155

Owner: David Doyonn.
Season: Late March to September.
Plane: Cessna 185 single-engine floatplane, three passengers.
Times: Three- to four-hour trips (about two to three hours flight time and one hour floating with whales) by arrangement.
Cost: $240 per air hour per plane.
Departs: Ketchikan Airport.
Refreshments: Picnic lunch provided.
Miscellaneous: Doyonn has 15 years' professional flying experience in Alaska, and has taken many biologists from Alaska's Fish and Game Department on marine mammal surveys.

RESOURCES

Alaskan Adventures Unlimited

403 Lincoln Street, #232
Sitka, AK 99835
907/747–5576, 800/770–5576; fax 907/747–5910

Susan Boyce serves as a booking agent for many Sitka charter operators, including most of the whale-watching and wildlife tour operations listed in this chapter. If you haven't reserved ahead, she can help you find available space.

Alaska Tourist Marketing Council
Department 601, P.O. Box 110801
Juneau, AK 99811–0801
907/465–2010; fax 907/465–2287

Division of Marine Highways
P.O. Box 25535
Juneau, AK 99802–5535
800/642–0066, 800/665–6414 (in Canada)

Gustavus Visitors Information
P.O. Box 167
Gustavus, AK 99826
907/697–2245

Ketchikan Information Center
131 Front Street
Ketchikan, AK 99901
907/225–6166, 800/770–2200; fax 907/225–4250

Kodiak Island Convention and Visitors Bureau
100 Marine Way
Kodiak, AK 99615
907/486–4782

Petersburg Visitor Center
P.O. Box 649
Petersburg, AK 99833
907/772–3646

Prince William Sound/Chugach National Forest Alaska Public Lands Information Center
605 West Fourth Avenue
Anchorage AK 99501
907/271–2737

Sitka Convention and Visitors Bureau
P.O. Box 1226
Sitka, AK 99835
907/747–5940; fax 907/747–3739

Viking Travel

P.O. Box 787
Petersburg, AK 99833
907/772–3818, 800/327–2571; fax 907/772–3940
Viking Travel books trips for several local whale-watching operators.

Wrangell Chamber of Commerce

Box 49
Wrangell, AK 99929
907/874–3901

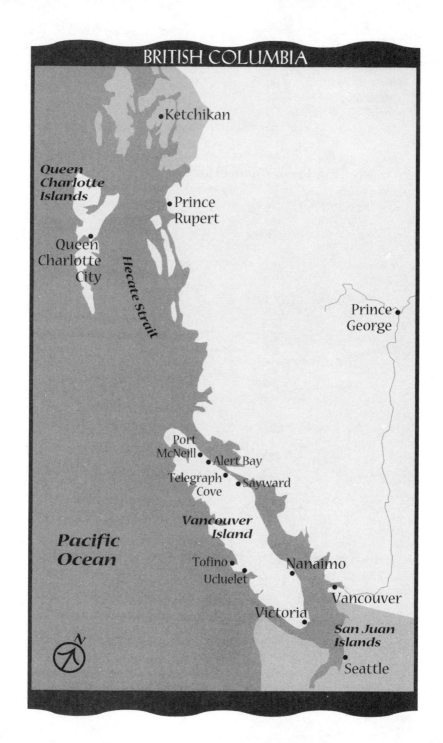

BRITISH COLUMBIA

•Ketchikan

Queen Charlotte Islands

•Prince Rupert

Queen Charlotte City

Hecate Strait

Prince• George

Port McNeill• •Alert Bay

Telegraph• •Sayward Cove

Vancouver Island

Pacific Ocean

Tofino• •Nanaimo Ucluelet

Victoria•

San Juan Islands

•Seattle

N

BRITISH COLUMBIA

Set between the Rocky Mountains and the Pacific Ocean, British Columbia is Canada's westernmost and wettest province. Like southeast Alaska just to the north, the coast of British Columbia is a labyrinth of hundreds of islands, inlets, fjords, straits, and sounds, surrounded by heavily wooded, mountainous terrain that is spectacular to behold. Much of the coast is accessible only by boat or floatplane.

Before the Europeans arrived in the eighteenth century, many native tribes thrived along the coast, supported by the abundant wildlife found in the water and on land. These people built their canoes, lodges, and totem poles out of the region's giant cedar trees. Many of the natural history trips listed in this chapter include visits to native cultural sites, some abandoned, others still inhabited.

Queen Charlotte Islands

Located 60 miles across the Hecate Strait from the northernmost stretch of British Columbia's mainland, the Queen Charlotte Islands are a remarkably beautiful and isolated region that's rich in marine wildlife. Only 4,000 people inhabit the 150 islands of the archipelago, which stretches out over 150 miles. The islands are famous for the cultural sites of the native Haida tribe, whose history in the region dates back 10,000 years. The abandoned Haida village of Ninstints at the southern end of the island chain has been declared a United Nations World Heritage Site.

Because the continental shelf drops into the ocean deeps just offshore, the west coast of the Queen Charlotte Islands offers unique whale-watching opportunities. It is possible, though not common, to see pelagic cetacean species such as sperm whales and beaked whales in these waters.

Humpbacks arrive on the east side of the islands in February, during the herring spawn, and remain in the area until fall; they are also seen to the west of the islands in summer. Gray whales migrate past both sides of the islands from March through June, and there may be a resident summer population here, just as there are off Vancouver Island and the Oregon coast. Orcas—both resident and transient pods—may be spotted any time of the year. A few minke whales may be seen, with individuals tending to remain in one area. Blue and fin whales are spotted infrequently on the west and occasionally, from mid-July through August, in the Hecate Strait off southeast Moresby Island. A Northern right whale was reportedly seen in August of 1988.

The last onshore whaling station in the region was located at Rose Harbor on Kunghit Island at the extreme southern tip of the Queen Charlottes. Most of the local humpback whale population was slaughtered and processed here in the 1950s and 1960s, which may explain why the number of humpbacks in the island chain remains low.

Dall's and harbor porpoises are commonly seen, as are Pacific white-sided dolphins, which often travel in large schools. Throughout the islands there are harbor seal and Steller's sea lion rookeries and haul-outs. Individual sea otters are occasionally sighted, but there is no established population yet.

North Vancouver Island

The quiet waters of Johnstone Strait off Vancouver Island's north shore are paradise for naturalists and anglers, offering superb orca watching and salmon fishing. Once home to tens of thousands of Kwagiulth natives, the area is now filled with abandoned village sites. A few are still inhabited, and there's a Kwagiulth cultural center in Alert Bay. Some consider the waters of Johnstone Strait to be the best place in the world to observe orcas, also known as killer whales. During the summer months, orcas can be observed almost daily. Robson Bight, a small bay along Johnstone Sound, contains "rubbing beaches," where orcas come in close to shore to slide along smooth pebbles. Robson Bight is now a protected ecological reserve, though it remains threatened by timber interests seeking to log the old-growth forests that make up the Bight's watershed.

Minkes are resident in the area but are rarely spotted on short whale-watching trips. Humpbacks and grays are seen occasionally. Dall's porpoises are common, as are harbor seals. Pacific white-sided dolphins and Steller's sea lions are also found in the area. Nesting bald eagles and marine birds are common.

The towns of Alert Bay, Port McNeill, and Telegraph Cove are home to several whale-watching operations. The area is served by commercial airlines and is about a six-hour drive up from Victoria, at the south end of Vancouver Island, or four and a half hours from Nanaimo, a terminus for ferries from Vancouver, BC.

West Vancouver Island

The rugged west coast of Vancouver Island is marked with bays and inlets, booming surf on Pacific beaches, and old-growth temperate rain forests. The 200-square-mile Pacific Rim National Park is a preserve for coastal wetlands, forests, and wildlife habitats. Whale-watching operations on the west coast are found in the fishing ports of Tofino and Ucluelet, which have large charter fishing fleets.

Beautiful Clayoquot Sound just north of Tofino is rich in marine life and surrounded by old-growth temperate rain forests. In recent years international attention has been focused on the area as environmentalists try to protect these forests and the sound's entire ecosystem from logging interests. The United Nations is considering turning the sound into a biosphere reserve.

The main event in this area is the northward gray whale migration, which peaks in March and April. Several dozen resident gray whales spend their summers feeding near Tofino and remain until the southward migration in late fall or early winter. Orcas were spotted often in 1994 but were scarce in other years. Minkes and humpbacks are sighted occasionally. Harbor porpoises, harbor seals, and California and Steller's sea lions are often seen. Dall's porpoises, minke whales, and elephant seals are sighted less frequently. There is an abundance of marine birds and nesting bald eagles in the area.

Huge basking sharks come into the waters behind Flores Island to give birth and are occasionally observed by people on natural history cruises.

Victoria

The capital of British Columbia and a famous tourist desination, Victoria is accessible to the northern end of the Puget Sound and the Gulf Islands featured in the Washington state chapter of this book.

ONSHORE WHALE-WATCHING SITES IN BRITISH COLUMBIA

Queen Charlotte Islands

(gray whale migration in May and June)
1. Rose Point/Rose Spit. Tow Hill Provincial Park, North Beach.
2. Skidegate Inlet, near Sandspit. Steps of museum in Second Beach.

Vancouver Island Outer Coast

(gray whale migration from November to April, but best from late February to June. Also, resident summer population of gray whales)
1. The headlands and bluffs along Highway 4 toward Tofino in the Long Beach area, particularly within the Pacific Rim National Park, Long Beach unit. Locations include Wickaninnish Bay, Schooner Cove, Green Point, Radar Hill summit, Quisitis Point, and Wya Point.
2. Along West Coast Trail between Bamfield and Port Renfrew (for experienced hikers).

All prices listed in this chapter are in **Canadian dollars**, unless otherwise noted. A sales tax will be added in most cases (7 percent for Canadians and 3.5 percent for visitors). When you make reservations, be sure to ask about currency, taxes, and exchange rates if you plan to pay in U.S. dollars.

Regional Extended Tour Operators

Blue Fjord Charters

P.O. Box 1450
Ladysmith, BC, V0R 2E0 Canada
604/245–8987

Captain: Mike Durbin.

Season: March and April—gray whale cruise; June to September—Johnstone Strait, Queen Charlotte Islands, and southeast Alaska.

Boat: *Blue Fjord*, a 65-foot classic wooden motor yacht and former RCMP vessel; 20 passengers for one-day trips, 10 passengers for multi-day trips.

Times: Full-day trips and multi-day live-aboard charters, usually one week long.

Cost: $1,200 a day for the whole boat.

Departs: Tofino (March and April), Port McNeill and points north (June to September).

Refreshments: Beverages and lunch on day trips; all meals on extended cruises.

Miscellaneous: Durbin has been working on marine wildlife conservation and touring since 1979, and has been a field officer with the Canadian Federal Fisheries Service and a tour naturalist in the Galapagos Islands. He's been offering tours on the *Blue Fjord* since 1986. On extended trips he likes to take clients to less-frequented areas. Boat is equipped with a hydrophone.

Bluewater Adventures

252 East First Street, #3
North Vancouver, BC, V7L 1B3 Canada
604/980–3800

Owner: Randy Burke.

Season: May to October.

Boat: S. V. *Island Roamer*, a 68-foot sailing ketch, 16 passengers.

Times: Five- to 11-day trips throughout the Pacific Northwest, including southeast Alaska, the Queen Charlotte Islands, Vancouver Island, and the San Juan and Gulf islands.

Cost: $875 to $2,500 per person (in U.S. currency).

Departs: Various ports in the Pacific Northwest.

Refreshments: Onboard meals and accommodations included.

Miscellaneous: In the business for over 20 years, Bluewater is one of the most experienced wildlife-tour operations in the Pacific Northwest. Zoos, museums, and other organizations often book passage for member cruises. Inflatables and kayaks are available. Expert naturalists accompany all trips.

Dolphin Charters

1007 Leneve Place
El Cerrito, CA 94530
510/527–9622

Captain: Ronn Storro-Patterson.

Season: Late May; September to October.

Boat: M. V. *Delphinus*, a 50-foot motor yacht designed for natural history cruises, 12 passengers.

Times: Five- to 9-night natural history expedition cruises around Vancouver Island and to Ketchikan, Alaska.

Cost: $1,595 to $2,795 per person (in U.S. currency).

Departs: Ketchikan, Port Hardy, Point Roberts, Friday Harbor.

Miscellaneous: Captain Storro-Patterson is a professional biologist and a former university professor. Dolphin Charters specializes in natural history cruises and education.

Ecosummer Canada Expeditions, Ltd.

1516 Duranleau Street
Vancouver, BC, V6H 3S4 Canada
604/669–7741, 800/688–8605 (within the U.S.), 800/465–8884 (within Canada)

Owner: Jim Allen.
Season: Mid-May to October.
Boats: *Ocean Light,* a 67-foot sailing cutter; eight passengers maximum; two-person sea kayaks, 10 guests per trip.
Times: Four- to 10-day wildlife cruises on the sailboat; two-day to two-week kayaking/camping trips in ocean kayaks.
Cost: Sailing cruises are $995 to $2,295 per person; kayaking trips are $245 to $2,295 per person.
Departs: Port McNeill, Queen Charlotte Islands, Gulf Islands, Western Vancouver Island.
Refreshments: All meals included.
Miscellaneous: With nearly 20 years in the business, Ecosummer is one of the most experienced of the local kayaking operators. A motor launch transports people and kayaks to departure locations.

Mapleleaf Adventures

2625 Muir Road, #19
Courtenay, BC, V9N 8S6 Canada
604/240–2420

Captain: Bryan Falconer.
Season: San Juan Islands, Washington (mid-March to mid-April); British Columbia's central coast (mid- to late April); Queen Charlotte Islands (May); southeast Alaska (June); Johnstone Strait (mid-September to mid-October).
Boat: S. V. *Mapleleaf,* a 92-foot classic wooden sailing schooner built in 1904 and completely restored, eight passengers.
Times: Four- to 11-day live-aboard cruises.
Cost: $750 to $2,300 per person.
Departs: Various ports in the Pacific Northwest and southeast Alaska.
Refreshments: All meals included.
Miscellaneous: Former bush pilot Bryan Falconer prefers to cruise the region's most remote and least-visited areas. Expert professional naturalists and marine biologists accompany all trips. Equipped with a hydrophone and two Zodiac inflatables.

Oceanic Society Expeditions

Fort Mason Center, Building E
San Francisco, CA 94123
415/441–1106, 800/326–7491 (U.S. only)

Season: July to September.
Boat: S. V. *Island Roamer,* a 68-foot sailing ketch, 16 passengers.
Times: Five- to 12-day cruises.
Cost: $1,250 to $2,990 per person (in U.S. currency).
Departs: Various regional ports.
Refreshments: All meals included.
Miscellaneous: A major nonprofit cetacean research and educa-
tion organization, Oceanic Society Expeditions has been offering
marine nature tours since 1972. Highly experienced naturalists
lead all cruises.

Special Expeditions, Inc.

720 Fifth Avenue
New York, NY 10019
212/765–7740, 800/762–0003

Founder: Sven-Olof Lindblad.
Season: August to September.
Boat: M. V. *Sea Bird* and M. V. *Sea Lion,* 152-foot custom-built
coastal cruise ships, 70 passengers each.
Times: Seven- to 12-day cruises from Alaska to British Columbia
and from Seattle to Vancouver Island.
Cost: $1,830 to $4,880 per person (in U.S. currency).
Departs: Sitka, Vancouver, Seattle.
Refreshments: All onboard meals included.
Miscellaneous: Special Expeditions has been offering wildlife cruis-
es worldwide since 1979, and is one of the most experienced
operators in the field. All cruises are staffed by experienced professional naturalists. Zodiacs are used to get closer to wildlife.

Queen Charlotte Islands Tour Operators

Anvil Cove Charters

Box 454
Queen Charlotte City, BC, V0T 1S0 Canada
604/559–8207, 800/668–4288

Captains: Keith and Barb Roswell.
Season: Scheduled multi-day cruises from May to November;
charters year-round.
Boat: *Anvil Cove,* a 53-foot steel-hulled sailing schooner, 12 pas-
sengers.
Times: Six- to 10-day cruises.

Cost: $175 a day per person.
Departs: Queen Charlotte City Dock.
Refreshments: All meals included.
Miscellaneous: Former commercial fishers, the Roswells have offered wildlife and cultural history tours for almost 20 years. They provide chartered tours to groups of professional scientists, biologists, and archaeologists for most of their season, but several scheduled cruises are available to the public each year, and sometimes places are available on the scientific cruises. The *Anvil Cove* is equipped with a hydrophone, kayaks, and a Zodiac inflatable.

Husband Charters

Box 733
Queen Charlotte City, BC, V0T 1S0 Canada
604/559–4582

Captain: Terry Husband.
Season: Mid-February to September.
Boat: *Kingii*, a 33-foot cabin cruiser, eight passengers.
Times: Full-day trips per demand; scheduled weeklong cruising/camping trips; multi-day charters.
Cost: $85 per person for day trips; multi-day cruises average $160 a day per person.
Departs: Queen Charlotte City Dock.
Refreshments: Beverages and hot lunch served on day trips; all meals provided on multi-day cruises.
Miscellaneous: Terry Husband, a fifth-generation Queen Charlotte Islander, is a former commercial fisherman. He and his wife, Charlotte, have been running marine wildlife and whale-watching trips since 1985. Multi-day cruises take in the west side and southern Haida cultural sites.

Queen Charlotte Adventures

Box 196
Queen Charlotte City, BC, V0T 1S0 Canada
604/559–8990, 800/668–4288

Captain: Mary Kelly.
Season: May to October.
Boats: *Anvil Cove,* a 53-foot steel-hulled sailing schooner, 12 passengers; two 28-foot powerboats; and two-person sea kayaks, eight people maximum per trip.
Times: Day trips and four- to six-day kayaking/camping tours.
Cost: $200 a day per person.
Departs: Queen Charlotte City Dock.
Refreshments: Beverages and lunch on day trips; all meals on extended trips.

Miscellaneous: Affiliated with Anvil Cove Charters, Queen Charlotte offers wildlife and whale-watching kayaking/camping trips guided by naturalists.

North Vancouver Island Tour Operators

Northern Lights Expeditions

6141 NE Bothell Way #101
Seattle, WA 98155
206/483–6396

Owner: David Arcese.
Season: Mid-June to late September.
Boats: Two-person sea kayaks, 13 people maximum per trip.
Times: Six-day kayaking/camping trips; two whale-watching trips per week; and a weekly "Mystery Tour" of secluded areas with a general wildlife orientation.
Cost: $950 per person, all-inclusive, for whale-watching trip; $899 per person for the "Mystery Tour" (in U.S. currency).
Departs: Telegraph Cove.
Refreshments: All meals included.
Miscellaneous: No one under 16 years old allowed. Northern Lights has been running sea kayaking trips on northern Vancouver Island for 12 years. Novices are welcome. Everything but sleeping bags and regular clothing is provided, including boots, waterproof overalls, hats, gloves, and outer gear. Three trained guides accompany each trip.

Robson Bight Charters

Box 99
Sayward, BC, V0P 1R0 Canada
604/282–3833

Captain: John Gansner.
Season: Mid-June to mid-October.
Boat: *Le Caique*, a 56-foot motor yacht, 30 passengers.
Times: All-day wildlife cruise leaves daily at 10 A.M.
Cost: $60 per person; $55 for seniors and children under 13.
Departs: Kelsey Bay, in Sayward.
Refreshments: Beverages, muffins, and cakes. Bring your own lunch.
Miscellaneous: Providing wildlife cruises for seven years. Experienced local captain and crew narrate. Equipped with a hydrophone.

Sea Smoke/Sail with the Whales

Box 483
Alert Bay, BC, V0N 1A0 Canada
604/974–5225, 800/668–ORCA or 6722 (within BC)

Owners: David and Maureen Towers.
Season: June to October.
Boats: *Tuan*, a 44-foot sailing cutter, 12 passengers; 24-foot Zodiac rigid inflatables, 12 passengers.
Times: Five- to six-hour sail cruises daily at 8 A.M. and 2 P.M.; three-hour Zodiac trips three times a day.
Cost: Cruise—$65 per person, $55 for children under 15; Zodiacs—$55 per person, $50 for children under 15.
Departs: Alert Bay, Alder Bay.
Refreshments: Cruise price includes elaborate meal and beverages; no food on the Zodiacs.
Miscellaneous: In operation since 1986. Naturalist/captain guides the Zodiac; full exposure clothing provided. David and Maureen narrate the sail cruise.

Stubbs Island Charters, Ltd.

P.O. Box 7
Telegraph Cove, BC, V0N 3J0 Canada
604/928–3117, 604/928–3185, 800/665–3066 (within BC)

Owners: Jim Borrowman, Bill and Donna McKay.
Season: Late June to mid-October.
Boats: Two 60-foot motor vessels: *Lukwa*, 48 passengers, and *Gikumi*, 30 passengers.
Times: Half-day trips leave daily at 9 A.M.; from mid-July to mid-September there's a second trip at 3 P.M.
Cost: $60 per person; $54 for seniors (65 and up); $50 for children under 13.
Departs: Telegraph Cove.
Refreshments: Meals available if ordered at check-in.
Miscellaneous: Active since 1980, the captains are highly experienced and knowledgeable. Hydrophones on board for listening to whales. Wheelchairs accommodated best on *Lukwa*.

Viking West Lodge and Charter

P.O. Box 113
Port McNeill, BC, V0N 2R0 Canada
604/956–3431, 800/889–ORCA or 6722

Owner: Dennis Richards.
Season: Mid-May to mid-October.
Boat: *Baroness*, a 24-foot cabin cruiser, six passengers; a 16-foot Zodiac rigid inflatable, four passengers.

Times: Private tours by reservation.

Cost: *Baroness*—$300 a person half-day, $500 full day; Zodiac—
$150 half-day, $300 full day. Lodging included on full-day
tours.

Departs: Port McNeill, Telegraph Cove.

Refreshments: Salmon barbecue lunch included on full-day trips.

Miscellaneous: Ten years' experience in wildlife trips. Hydrophone and recording equipment on all cruises. Fishing included.

Wayward Wind Charters

P.O. Box 300
Sointula, BC, V0N 3E0 Canada
604/973–6307

Owners: John and Vilma Gamble.

Season: Mid-June to early October.

Boat: *Wayward Wind,* a 28-foot sailboat, eight passengers.

Times: Eight-hour trip daily.

Cost: $65 per person; $45 for seniors and children ages 5 to 12.

Departs: Sointula.

Refreshments: Lunch included.

Miscellaneous: Fifteen years' experience; the skipper serves as a
naturalist.

West Vancouver Island Tour Operators

Chinook Charters

450 Campbell Street
Box 501
Tofino, BC, V0R 2Z0 Canada
604/725–3431, 800/665–3646

Owner: Mike Hansen.

Captains: Earl Thomas and Wilfred Atleo.

Season: March to October for scheduled whale-watching trips;
year-round for charters and special events.

Boats: *Chinook-Key,* a 32-foot custom-built whale-watching boat,
12 passengers; *Whale's Tale,* a 25-foot Zodiac, 12 passengers.

Times: Several two- to three-hour trips daily, usually at 9 A.M.,
noon, and 3 P.M.; ask about sunset cruises.

Cost: $35 per person; $30 for seniors (65 and up) and students;
$20 for children 6 to 12; free for children under 6.

Departs: Tofino Harbor.

Refreshments: Bring your own provisions.

Miscellaneous: In the whale-watching business since 1991.
Narration from experienced local captains. Speedy boats get
out to the whales quickly. Wheelchairs accommodated on
Chinook-Key.

Jamie's Whaling Station/Ocean Pacific Charters

606 Campbell Street
P.O. Box 590
Tofino, BC, V0R 2Z0 Canada
604/725–3919, 800/667–9913 (within BC)

Owner: Jamie Bray.

Season: February 15 to October.

Boats: *Lady Selkirk*, a 65-foot whale-watching motor vessel with four viewing decks, 47 passengers; three Zodiac rigid inflatables, 19 to 23 feet, 8 to 12 passengers.

Times: *Lady Selkirk* (two hours) departs daily at 11 A.M. and 1:30 P.M. in March and April; *Lady Selkirk* (three hours) departs daily at 10 A.M. and 1:30 P.M. from May to October; Zodiacs (two hours) depart daily at 9:30 A.M., noon, and 3 P.M. from March to October.

Cost: *Lady Selkirk*—$60 per person, $55 for seniors (65 and up), $30 for children 6 to 16, $15 for children under 6, infants free; Zodiacs—$40 per person, $25 for children under 16 (no one under 6 allowed).

Departs: Tofino Whaling Wharf.

Refreshments: *Lady Selkirk* has a full galley/bar. Nothing available on the Zodiacs.

Miscellaneous: In operation since 1982. Experienced skippers. Wheelchairs accommodated on *Lady Selkirk*. Waterproof flotation cruising suits provided for Zodiac passengers. Guaranteed whale sightings or the next trip is free.

R&S Tours

Box 213
Tofino, BC, V0R 2Z0 Canada
604/725–3958

Owners: Rod and Sharon Palm.

Season: March to October; year-round by request.

Boat: *Eco*, a 24-foot Boston Whaler, 12 passengers.

Times: Two-and-a-half-hour trips depart daily at 10 A.M., 2 P.M., and 6 P.M.

Cost: $40 per person; $35 for seniors (65 and up) and students; $25 for children under 13.

Departs: Tofino Harbor, Way West Marina.

Refreshments: Bring your own.

Miscellaneous: Providing whale-watching tours since 1988. Skipper/naturalist Rod Palm has over 15 years' experience in marine wildlife research. Cruiser suits are provided for all passengers.

Remote Passages

568 Campbell Street
P.O. Box 634
Tofino, BC, V0R 2Z0 Canada
604/725–3330, 604/725–3163, 800/666–9833 (within BC)

Owner: Don Travers.

Season: March to October.

Boats: Nineteen- to 24-foot Zodiac rigid inflatables, 8 to 12 passengers.

Times: "Whale Watching Plus" (three hours) departs daily at 9 A.M., noon, and 3 P.M.; "Hot Springs Explorer" (six to seven hours) departs in the early afternoon.

Cost: "Whale Watching Plus"—$40 per person, $35 for students, $20 for children 3 to 11, free for children under 3; "Hot Springs Explorer"—$60 per person, $55 for students, $40 for children 3 to 11, free for children under 3.

Departs: Meares Landing, Tofino Harbor.

Refreshments: Bring your own.

Miscellaneous: Operating since 1985. All skippers are naturalists. Dry cruiser suits provided to all passengers. "Hot Springs" tours take visitors to thermal rock pools overlooking Clayoquot Sound about 20 miles north of Tofino, where they can explore a temperate rain forest and soak in the pools before they begin watching for whales.

Sea Trek Tours

441-B Campbell Street
Box 627
Tofino, BC, V0R 2Z0 Canada
604/725–4412

Captain: Midavaine Didier.

Season: March to October.

Boat: A 27-foot high-speed Bertram, 12 passengers.

Times: Two-and-a-half-hour whale-watching trip every morning; six-and-a-half-hour whale-watching/hot springs tour in the afternoon.

Cost: Morning—$35 per person, $30 for seniors and students, $20 for children 5 to 12; afternoon—$55 per person, $50 for seniors and students, $30 for children 5 to 12; children under 5 free (one per family).

Departs: Tofino Harbor, Fourth Street Dock

Refreshments: Bring your own.

Miscellaneous: In business since 1994, but principals have been working in the whale/marine wildlife tour industry in Tofino for several years. Trips narrated by experienced skipper.

Subtidal Adventures

Box 78
1950 Peninsula Road
Ucluelet, BC, V0R 3A0 Canada
604/726–7336

Captain: Brian Congdon.
Season: March to September.
Boats: *Dixie IV*, a 36-foot cruiser and former Coast Guard lifeboat, 12 passengers; *Contender*, a 24-foot Polaris rigid inflatable, 12 passengers.
Times: March and April—daily at 8:30 A.M., 9:30 A.M., 11 A.M., and 2 P.M. (two hours on *Contender*, three hours on *Dixie IV*). May to September—"Broken Islands Nature Tour and Whale Watch" (four hours) daily at 8 A.M. on *Contender* and 1:30 P.M. on *Dixie IV*.
Cost: March and April—$35 per person, $20 for children 6 to 12, $10 for children under 6; May to September, morning—$55 per person, $35 for children 6 to 12, $25 for children under 6; May to September, afternoon—$39 per person, $20 for children 6 to 12, $10 for children under 6.
Departs: Ucluelet Boat Basin.
Refreshments: Bring your own.
Miscellaneous: Captain Congdon has been running whale/ wildlife cruises since 1978. Cruiser flotation suits are provided on *Contender*.

Victoria Tour Operators

Canadian Princess Resort

Oak Bay Marine Group
1327 Beach Drive
Victoria, BC, V8S 2N4 Canada
604/726–7771, 800/663–7090

Season: Mid-March to mid-April.
Boats: Eight 43- to 50-foot motor cruisers, 14 to 22 passengers.
Times: Three-hour trip departs daily at 9 A.M.
Cost: $35 per person; $20 for children under 13; family rates available.
Departs: Canadian Princess Resort Dock on Barclay Sound, Ucluelet.
Refreshments: Coffee and drinks.
Miscellaneous: Packages that include whale watching, resort lodging, and bus tours from Vancouver and Victoria are available. In the business since 1986. Experienced skippers narrate trips. Wheelchairs accommodated.

Sea Coast Expeditions

1655 Ash Road
Victoria, BC, V8N 2T2 Canada
604/477–1818

Owner: Alex Rhodes.
Season: April to October.
Boats: Fleet of 23-foot custom-built Zodiac rigid inflatables, 6 to 12 passengers.
Times: Two-hour trip daily at 1 P.M. (April and October); several two- and three-hour trips daily (May to September).
Cost: Three hours—$70 per person, $45 for children under 17; two hours—$50 per person, $30 for children under 17.
Departs: Ocean Pointe Resort, Victoria.
Refreshments: None served.
Miscellaneous: Founded in 1987. High-speed, hydrophone-equipped Zodiacs. Full-length flotation cruiser suits supplied to all passengers. Two knowledgeable professionals crew each trip.

RESOURCES

Alert Bay Tourist Information Centre

P.O. Box 28
Alert Bay, BC, V0N 1A0 Canada
604/284–5213

Maritime Museum/Whale Center

411 Campbell Street
P.O. Box 393
Tofino, BC, V0R 2Z0 Canada
604/725–3163, 604/725–2132

Scientific and artistic displays, photographs, and artifacts related to whales and whaling, European exploration and settlement, and native cultures on the west coast of Vancouver Island. They offer guided tours, lectures, and films. There's a gift shop and a reservation service for whale-watching charters. Open early March to mid-October, daily 9 A.M. to 5 P.M. Admission is free.

Pacific Rim Whale Festival

Tofino, Ucluelet, and the Pacific Rim National Park Reserve sponsor this annual celebration of the gray whale migration. (In 1996 the festival runs from March 16 to April 8.) There are special events such as the "Great Geoduck Competition," lectures, guided whale-spotting hikes, concerts, theatrical shows, and more. For brochures and assistance with reservations, contact the information centers for Tofino or Ucluelet (listed below).

Port McNeill Tourist Information Centre

P.O. Box 129
Port McNeill, BC, V0N 2R0 Canada
604/956–3131

Queen Charlotte Islands Travel Infocentre

Box 337
3922 Highway 33
Queen Charlotte, BC, V0T 1S0 Canada
604/559–4742

Tofino Chamber of Commerce

Box 476
121 Third Street
Tofino, BC, V0R 2Z0 Canada
604/725–3414

Tourism British Columbia

Parliament Buildings
Victoria, BC, V8V 1X4 Canada
604/387–1642, 800/663–6000

Ucluelet Travel Infocentre

Box 468
Ucluelet, BC, V0R 3A0 Canada
604/726–4641

Vancouver Public Aquarium

P.O. Box 3232
Stanley Park
Vancouver, BC, V6B 3X8 Canada
604/685–3364, 604/682–1118 (recorded message)

One of the finest public aquariums on the West Coast, the Vancouver Public Aquarium has orcas and belugas among its exhibits. Lectures, films, and research activities. Open daily year-round 10 A.M. to 5:30 P.M. (9:30 A.M. to 8 P.M. in July and August). Admission: $9.50 for adults, $8.25 for seniors and teens; $6.25 for children 5 to 12; free for children 4 and under.

Victoria Travel Infocentre

812 Wharf Street
Victoria, BC, V8W 1T3 Canada
604/382–2127

The Wickaninnish Centre

Pacific Rim National Park
Box 280
Ucluelet, BC, V0R 3A0 Canada
604/726–4212 (April to November), 604/726–7721 (off-season)

Overlooking Wickaninnish Bay and the Pacific Ocean, this interpretive center for the Pacific Rim National Park has exhibits, displays, and films on the natural and cultural history of the area. Open daily from mid-March to mid-September; call for hours. Admission is free.

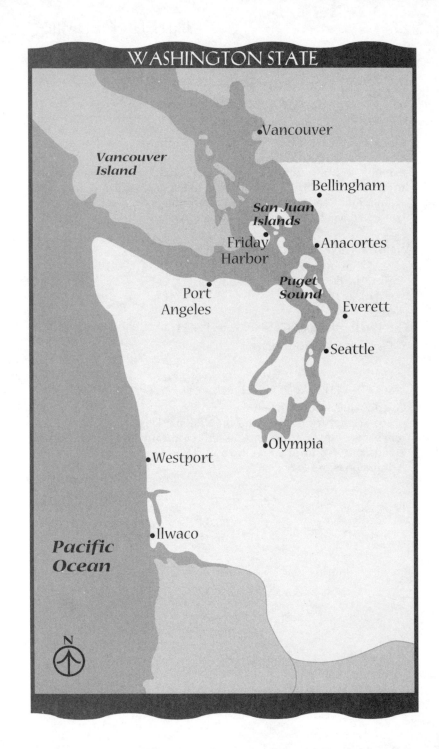

WASHINGTON STATE

Vancouver

Vancouver
Island

Bellingham

San Juan
Islands

Friday
Harbor

Anacortes

Puget
Sound

Port
Angeles

Everett

Seattle

Olympia

Westport

Ilwaco

Pacific
Ocean

N

6

WASHINGTON
STATE

Whale-watching opportunities in Washington state abound in two separate areas, each with its own distinct flavor. In the protected waters of the San Juan Islands in Puget Sound, resident pods of orcas and seasonally resident minke whales are viewed by thousands of people from May through September. And every spring, gray whales pass along the outer Pacific coast on their annual migration, and cruise activity is centered around the town of Westport. Pinnipeds are seen in both areas.

PUGET SOUND

San Juan Islands

Some of the best whale and marine mammal watching in North America can be found to the north of Seattle, in the usually placid waters of the San Juan Islands in Puget Sound. One big draw for many whale watchers: because the inland waters are so calm, seasickness is not a problem here.

These waters are home to three resident orca pods, which are observed easily from May through September. Orcas can be individually identified by their fin shape, scars, and unique color patches. Every orca in these three pods has been identified and was subsequently assigned a name, number, and even a nickname. Their relationships, ancestry, and behavior are studied intensely by legions of scientists and amateurs. When whale watching in the San Juans, expect your guides to be on a first-name basis with the whales. You might hear them say things like, "Oh, that's Shala, you know, the 'Teen Angel.' He's Ino's older brother."

Between 1964 and 1975, nearly all the orcas around the San Juan Islands were trapped at least once by collectors for museums, aquariums, and sideshows. Some 60 animals were removed from the population, and the rest were released, leaving only 68 orcas, according to a census taken in the late 1970s. During a careful census in 1993, 98 animals were counted. In 1994, to the dismay of many, four were missing and are presumed dead. Some were reported as looking sick and emaciated before they disappeared.

Small transient pods of orcas are also seen in the area as they move up and down the coast. Throughout the Pacific Northwest an interesting distinction has been noted between resident and transient pods: the resident pods almost exclusively eat salmon and other large fish, while the transient pods usually seek warm-blooded prey such as seals, sea lions, dolphins, and porpoises.

There is a fairly stable local population of minke whales in the islands, a number of which have been individually identified by their dorsal fin shape, scars, and markings and given names like Ed, Bubbles, Stormy, and Booker.

Dall's and harbor porpoises, harbor seals, and California and Steller's sea lions are fairly common. Gray whales are frequently seen in the greater Puget Sound region. Some venture in during their migration, and then continue north; others remain as a resident summer population. Pacific white-sided dolphins and elephant seals are seen less often.

Whale watching has become so popular out of Friday Harbor that at the peak of the season there may be well over a hundred craft following a single pod of orcas. Fortunately, it doesn't seem to bother the local whales, according to a recent study. Most of the cruise operators listed in this chapter belong to a cooperative whale-spotting network, which greatly increases their chances of seeing whales on any given day. They recently joined together to form Whalewatch Operators Association North West, an organization that promotes responsible and cooperative whale-watching among tour operators in an effort to create a better experience for their passengers. When you make reservations, ask if the operator is a member.

Seattle Area

Located on Washington's mainland coast in the greater Seattle area, Bellingham, Anacortes, and Everett offer whale-watching cruises to the San Juan Islands. During peak summer season this can be a big plus because you don't have to take a ferry out first. The drawback is that the cruises take much longer to get out to the islands and back, leaving less time for pure whale watching.

PACIFIC COAST

Westport

Westport is located on Washington's Pacific coast, roughly 110 miles south of Cape Flattery and the northern tip of the Olympic Peninsula. It lies at the tip of its own small peninsula that forms the southern entrance to the large natural bay of Grays Harbor just a two-and-a-half-hour drive from Seattle.

Westport's whale-watching season runs from March to May, when gray whales pass just outside the harbor on their northward migration. At the peak of the season, you will most likely see whales, which often approach drifting boats that have cut their props. Many whales spy hop for a better look, some rub against boat bottoms, while others surface right next to the boats and allow people to reach out and pet them. The few "friendlies" that exhibit this behavior tend to stay in the area anywhere from several days to longer than a week.

Whales enter the bay regularly during the migration. On the frequent occasions when the seas outside are rough, tour boats can remain in the bay and still find whales, as well as a wealth of other marine wildlife.

Minke whales and orcas, which are more common in the summer months, are occasionally sighted. Harbor porpoises are common, but Dall's porpoises are not. On offshore fishing trips that go 40 to 50 miles out, sperm whales, humpbacks, and blues are occasionally spotted, but the odds of seeing them on any given trip are quite small. Harbor seals and California and Steller's sea lions are seen regularly.

Ilwaco

Ilwaco is the southernmost town on Washington's Pacific coast. In the spring, a few boats from the Port of Ilwaco charter sportfishing fleet take people out on request to view the passing gray whale migration. Trips are scheduled according to demand, the weather, the waves, and the tides. Seas are often rough, so be sure to take your seasickness medicine.

San Juan Islands

(orcas, minke whales, and Dall's porpoises)

1. San Juan Island: Along West Side Road and, primarily, Lime Kiln Point State Park. Cattle Point on the southeast tip of the island.
2. Stuart Island: Turn Point on the northern tip.

Puget Sound, mainland shore

(gray whale migration from April to June)

1. Kayak Point Regional Park, Port Susan Bay.

Pacific Coast

(gray whale migration from late October to December and return migration February to May. Best viewing from March to May). Shore points from north to south:

1. Cape Flattery.
2. Shi Shi Beach Bluffs.
3. Cape Alava (Flattery Rocks National Refuge).
4. La Push.
5. Olympic National Park.
6. Destruction Island Overlook.
7. Kalaloch.
8. Point Grenville.
9. Moclips-Pacific Beach.
10. Westport.
11. North Head Light/Cape Disappointment.

PUGET SOUND TOUR OPERATORS

San Juan Islands Tour Operators

Bon Accord

P.O. Box 472
Friday Harbor, WA 98250
206/378–5921

Captain: Rick Karon.
Season: May to mid-October; off-season per demand.
Boat: *Bon Accord*, a 30-foot trawler, six passengers.
Times: Five- to six-hour trip daily at noon.
Cost: $55 per person.
Departs: Friday Harbor.

Refreshments: Bring your own.

Miscellaneous: Captain Karon, a certified naturalist with the Friday Harbor Whale Museum, has been offering whale-watching cruises since 1989.

Deer Harbor Charters

P.O. Box 303
Deer Harbor, WA 98243
206/376–5989, 800/544–5758

Captain: Tom Averna.
Season: April to October.
Boat: *Yaki Taki*, 36 feet, 15 passengers.
Times: Four-hour cruise daily at 9 A.M. and 2 P.M.
Cost: $40 per person; $35 for seniors (65 and up); $25 for children under 13.
Departs: Deer Harbor.
Refreshments: Snacks and drinks sold on board.
Miscellaneous: In operation since 1990. Naturalist accompanies all trips. Wheelchairs accommodated.

Fairweather Water Taxi and Tours

P.O. Box 1273
Friday Harbor, WA 98250
206/378–2826

Captain: Lisa Lamb.
Season: Year-round per demand.
Boat: *Way To Go*, a 30-foot Russian-built hydrofoil, six passengers.
Times: Negotiable.
Cost: $60 an hour for up to six people.
Departs: Roche Harbor (or they can pick you up at any harbor in the San Juan Islands).
Refreshments: Bring your own.
Miscellaneous: Captain Lamb has been operating her water taxi and wildlife tour service since 1988. She will drop off and pick up campers at state parks and campgrounds in the San Juan Islands that are not served by regular ferries. Some of these islands offer excellent whale and wildlife viewing.

Orcas Island Eclipse Charters

P.O. Box 290
Orcas, WA 98280
206/376–4663, 800/376–6566

Captain: Dan Wilk.
Season: Late May to mid-October; weekends per demand in off-season.

Boat: *Eclipse I,* a 42-foot charter boat, 36 passengers.
Times: Four-and-a-half-hour trip daily at 11:30 A.M.
Cost: $42 per person; $32 for children under 13.
Departs: Orcas Ferry Landing.
Refreshments: Bring your own.
Miscellaneous: In operation since 1991. Member of whale-sighting network. Wheelchairs accommodated.

San Juan Boat Rentals and Tours

P.O. Box 2281
Friday Harbor, WA 98250
206/378–3499, 800/232–6722

Captain: Darrell Roberts.
Season: Mid-May to September; year-round wildlife cruises per demand.
Boats: *Double Header,* 26 feet, 6 passengers; *Blackfish,* a 30-foot custom-built whale-watching boat, 15 passengers.
Times: Three-and-a-half- to four-hour cruises usually depart daily at 10 A.M. and 2 P.M.; call for schedule.
Cost: $40 per person; $25 for children 6 to 12.
Departs: Friday Harbor.
Refreshments: Bring your own.
Miscellaneous: Operating since 1989; naturalist accompanies trips on *Blackfish.*

Sea Quest Expeditions/Zoetic Research

Zoetic Research
P.O. Box 2424
Friday Harbor, WA 98250
206/378–5767

Contact: Mark Lewis, Expedition Director.
Season: May to October.
Boats: Two-person sea kayaks, 12 guests maximum per trip.
Times: One- to five-day kayaking/camping trips.
Cost: $49 per person for a one-day trip; $189 to $399 per person for multi-day trips.
Departs: Friday Harbor Ferry Terminal.
Refreshments: Breakfast and dinner included on multi-day trips; bring your own snacks for lunch.
Miscellaneous: Zoetic Research is a nonprofit environmental research and education organization. Research biologists accompany every trip. No previous kayaking experience is necessary, but you must be physically fit.

Western Prince Cruises

P.O. Box 418
Friday Harbor, WA 98250
206/378–5315, 800/757–ORCA (6722)

Captains: Bob and Jean Van Leuven.
Season: May to October.
Boat: *Western Prince*, 46 feet, 35 passengers.
Times: May and October (Wednesday, Friday, Saturday, and Sunday); June and September (Wednesday to Sunday); July and August (closed Tuesday). Four-hour trip at 1 or 2 P.M. (occasionally at 9 A.M.).
Cost: $43 per person; $31 for children 4 to 12.
Departs: Friday Harbor.
Refreshments: Coffee, drinks, and snacks (no sandwiches) sold on board.
Miscellaneous: Friday Harbor's first tour operator has been in business since 1987. Full-time naturalist accompanies trips.

Seattle Area Tour Operators

Island Mariner Cruises

#5 Harbor Esplanade
Bellingham, WA 98225
206/743–8866

Owner: David Seymour.
Season: June 3 to September 10.
Boat: *Island Caper*, a 110-foot touring vessel, 110 passengers.
Times: Seven-hour "Whale Search" cruise departs Saturday and Sunday at 10:30 A.M. (Tuesday and Thursday also in July and August).
Cost: $45 per person; $40 for seniors (62 and up); $35 for children under 16.
Departs: Squalicum Harbor in Bellingham.
Refreshments: Full galley on board; hot and cold food sold.
Miscellaneous: Running cruises in the San Juan Islands since 1962. Member of whale spotting service. Naturalist accompanies all trips. Hydrophones pick up whale sounds. Wheelchair accessible.

Mosquito Fleet

1724F West Marine Drive
Everett, WA 98201–2087
206/252–6800, 800/380–ORCA (6722)

Contact: Katherine, Office Manager.
Captain/Owner: Martin H. Behr.

Season: May 27 to September 17 (peak season); May 6 to May 21 and September 23 to October 29 (value season).

Boat: M. V. *Flyer,* a 90-foot V-hulled cruise boat, 149 passengers.

Times: Nine-hour trip leaves daily at 8:30 A.M. in peak season; weekends only in value season.

Cost: Peak season—$69 per person, $59 for seniors (65 and up), $49 for under 18; value season—$49 per person, $44 for seniors (65 and up), $39 for under 18; children under 3 free.

Departs: Everett Marina Village, Port of Everett.

Refreshments: Full galley on board; hot and cold food for sale.

Miscellaneous: In operation since 1992, Mosquito Fleet stresses that the "San Juan Islands Sea Life" cruises are more than just whale-watching trips. They stop at major seabird rookeries, and a marine biologist is on board to narrate and answer questions.

Pacific Cruises

355 Harris Avenue, Suite 104
Bellingham, WA 98225
360/738–8099, 800/443–4552

Captain/Owner: Drew Schmidt.

Season: Mid-May to mid-October.

Boat: M. V. *Victoria Star,* an 80-foot cruise boat, 300 passengers.

Times: Departs Bellingham daily at 9:30 A.M. and arrives in Victoria at 12:30 P.M. Leaves Victoria at 4 P.M. and reaches Bellingham at 7 P.M.

Cost: $74 per person; $37 for children 6 to 17; children under 6 free.

Departs: Bellingham Cruise Terminal.

Refreshments: Full galley and bar.

Miscellaneous: In operation since 1987. A naturalist accompanies all trips, and binoculars are provided. Videos on whales and natural history are played on board. Fully accessible to wheelchairs.

Seattle Aquarium Whale-Watching Tours

Pier 59, Waterfront Park
Seattle, WA 98101
206/386–4300

Season: June to Labor Day.

Boat: *Spirit of Saratoga Passage,* 50 feet, 40 passengers.

Times: Eight-hour "Orca Search" cruise on Monday, Tuesday, Saturday, and Sunday leaves at 10 A.M. (weekends only in June).

Cost: $65 per person; $60 for children under 13.

Departs: Cap Sante Marina in Anacortes.

Refreshments: Food available on board.

Miscellaneous: The aquarium has been running its whale-watching cruises for more than 10 years. Three naturalists accompany each trip.

PACIFIC COAST TOUR OPERATORS

Westport Tour Operators

Bran Lee Charters

2467 Westhaven Drive
Westport, WA 98595,
360/268–9177, 800/562–0163

Captain/Owner: Dorothy Parker.

Season: March to May.

Boats: *Hop 2,* a 55-foot charter boat, 30 passengers; *Dorothy J.,* a 65-foot charter boat, 50 passengers.

Times: Two- to two-and-a-half-hour cruises depart daily at 11 A.M. and 2 P.M.

Cost: $17.50 per person; $10 for children under 13.

Departs: Westport Marina.

Refreshments: Bring your own.

Miscellaneous: Offering whale-watching cruises for more than 15 years. Knowledgeable skippers narrate. Wheelchairs accommodated.

Cachalot Charters

P.O. Box 348
Westport, WA 98595
360/268–0323, 800/356–0323

Captain: Dave Camp.

Season: March to early May.

Boats: *Discovery,* a 55-foot sportfisher, 30 passengers; *King Pin,* a 48-foot sportfisher, 20 passengers.

Times: Two-and-a-half-hour cruises depart Saturday and Sunday at 11 A.M. and 2 P.M.; depart weekdays at noon.

Cost: $24.95 per person; $12.50 for children under 13.

Departs: Westport Marina.

Refreshments: Coffee.

Miscellaneous: Offering whale-watching cruises since 1982. Captain Camp is the naturalist/narrator. Wheelchairs accommodated.

Coho Charters

P.O. Box 1087
Westport, WA 98595
360/268–0111, 800/562–0177

Captains: Vince Putze and Doc Uhlig.
Season: March to May.
Boats: *Shenandoah,* a 43-foot charter boat, 30 passengers; *Outer Limits,* a 65-foot charter boat, 49 passengers.
Times: Two-and-a-half-hour cruise departs daily at 11 A.M. and 2 P.M.
Cost: $19.50 per person; $12.50 for children under 13.
Departs: Westport Marina.
Refreshments: Coffee and snacks.
Miscellaneous: Experienced captains narrate. Wheelchairs accommodated.

Deep Sea Charters

P.O. Box 1115
Westport, WA 98595
360/268–9300, 800/562–0151

Owner: Ken Bowe.
Season: March to May.
Boats: Six 36- to 55-foot sportfishing boats, 6 to 30 passengers.
Times: Two- to two-and-a-half-hour trips twice daily; schedule depends on tide.
Cost: $25 per person; $15 for children under 14; group discounts available.
Departs: Westport Marina.
Refreshments: Coffee.
History: In the whale-watching business for more than 10 years. A biologist-narrated film and lecture is provided onshore before departure. Experienced captains narrate on board.

Neptune Charters

P.O. Box 426
Westport, WA 98595
360/268–0124, 800/562–0425

Captain/Owner: Bill Hoffman.
Season: March to mid-June.
Boats: Fleet of sportfishing boats, 40 to 85 feet, 15 to 80 passengers.
Times: Two-and-a-half-hour cruise daily at 10 A.M. and 1 P.M.
Cost: $19.50 per person; $12.50 for children under 13.
Departs: Westport Marina.

Refreshments: Coffee; largest boat has full galley.

Miscellaneous: Whale-watching cruises since 1978. Gray whale video shown onshore before departure. Experienced captains narrate. Wheelchairs accommodated.

Northwest Educational Tours

737 Eighth Avenue
Aberdeen, WA 98520
360/532–6988

Owner: Dr. John Smith.

Season: March to May 15.

Boats: Various charter boats.

Times: Two-and-a-half-hour cruise departs Saturday and Sunday at 10 A.M. and 2 P.M.

Cost: $23 per person; $12.50 for children under 13.

Departs: Westport Marina.

Miscellaneous: Dr. Smith has been leading whale-watching tours out of Westport since 1982. A Ph.D. in zoology who taught fisheries science for over 30 years, Smith also gives gray whale lectures on the weekends at the Maritime Museum.

Ocean Charters

P.O. Box 548
Westport, WA, 98585
360/268–9144, 800/562–0105

Owner: Cliff Beatty.

Season: March to June.

Boats: Four 54- to 80-foot boats, 30 to 110 passengers.

Times: Two-and-a-half-hour cruise departs daily at 11 A.M. and 2 P.M.

Cost: $19.95 per person; $12 for children under 13.

Departs: Westport Marina.

Refreshments: Coffee; largest boat has full galley and bar.

Miscellaneous: Taped narration. New owners took over in 1986. Wheelchairs accommodated.

Pacific Cruises

355 Harris Avenue, Suite 104
Bellingham, WA 98225
360/738–8099, 800/443–4552

Captain/Owner: Drew Schmidt.

Season: March and April.

Boat: M. V. *Victoria Star*, an 80-foot cruise boat, 300 passengers.

Times: Two-and-a-half-hour cruise departs Thursday through Sunday at 11 A.M.

Cost: $24 per person; $12 for children 6 to 17; children under 6 free.
Departs: Westport Marina.
Refreshments: Full galley and bar.
Miscellaneous: Naturalist on board. Binoculars provided. Onboard videos on whales and natural history. Fully wheelchair accessible.

Seattle Aquarium Whale-Watching Tours

Pier 59, Waterfront Park
Seattle, WA 98101
206/386–4300

Season: March 18 to April 30.
Boats: Sportfishing fleet at Salmon Charters.
Times: Three-hour trip leaves Saturday and Sunday around 1 P.M., depending on tides.
Cost: $28 per person; $20 for children under 13.
Departs: Westport Marina.
Refreshments: Coffee.
Miscellaneous: Naturalist on board. Pre-trip lectures on weeknights at the Seattle Aquarium and on the weekends in Westport.

Travis Charters

P.O. Box 1664
Westport, WA 98955
360/268–9140, 800/648–1520

Captain: Geoff Grillo.
Season: March to May.
Boat: *Advantage*, 56 feet, 28 passengers.
Times: Two-and-a-half-hour cruise departs daily at 11 A.M. and 2 P.M.
Cost: $22 per person; $16 for children under 16.
Departs: Westport Marina.
Refreshments: Coffee available.
Miscellaneous: Captain Grillo, who has 12 years' whale-watching experience, narrates. The owners stress that Travis Charters provides not just whale watching but a complete wildlife tour of Gray Harbor, including pinnipeds, marine birds, and other species. Wheelchairs accommodated.

Westport Charters

P.O. Box 546
Westport, WA 98595
360/268–9120

Owner: Mark Cedergreen.
Season: March to May.
Boats: Six 40- to 50-foot boats, 16 to 28 passengers.
Times: Two-and-a-half-hour cruise departs daily at 10 A.M. and 1 P.M.
Cost: $24 per person; $15 for children under 16; group discounts available.
Departs: Westport Marina.
Refreshments: Coffee available.
Miscellaneous: In business since 1986. Skippers narrate. Wheelchairs accommodated. Bed-and-breakfast/whale-watching packages available.

Ilwaco Tour Operator

Pacific Salmon Charters

P.O. Box 519
Ilwaco, WA 98624
206/642–3466, 800/831–2695

Owner: Milt Gudgell.
Season: March to mid-April (by request).
Boats: Seven 26- to 56-foot charter fishing vessels, 6 to 30 passengers.
Times: Three-hour trips, depending on demand, tides, and weather.
Cost: $45 per person; group discounts available.
Departs: Port of Ilwaco.
Refreshments: Coffee.
Miscellaneous: In the charter business for more than 30 years; offering whale-watching trips since 1991.

RESOURCES

Orcas Island Chamber of Commerce
206/376–8888

San Juan Island Bed-and-Breakfast Association
206/378–3030

San Juan Islands Visitor Information Service
P.O. Box 65
Lopez Island, WA 98261
206/468–3663

Seattle Aquarium
Pier 59, Waterfront Park
Seattle, WA 98101
206/386–4320
In addition to its extensive exhibits, the Seattle Aquarium provides tours, lectures, research, and educational programs, and sponsors whale-watching trips in Puget Sound and Westport. Open year-round; call for hours. Admission fee.

Washington State Tourism Division
P.O. Box 42500
Olympia, WA, 98504–2500
206/753–5600

Westport/Grayland Chamber of Commerce
P.O. Box 306
Westport, WA 98595–0306
360/268–9422, 800/345–6223; fax 360/268–1990

Westport Maritime Museum
2201 Westhaven Drive
P.O. Box 1074
Westport, WA 98595–1074
360/268–0078
Located in a former Coast Guard station and operated by the Westport–South Beach Historical Society, the museum provides exhibits and educational programs relating to the Coast Guard, the local whaling and maritime industries, and the region's natural history, particularly that of marine mammals. Skeletons of

some marine mammals are displayed in a house on the grounds. On weekends during the prime gray whale migration season (March through May), the museum presents slide shows on whales and lectures by Dr. John Smith (of Northwest Educational Tours) daily at 9 A.M. and noon. Days and hours vary by season, so call ahead. Admission free; donations requested.

The Whale Museum

> 62 First Street North
> Friday Harbor, WA 98250
> 206/378–4710

If you're in Friday Harbor, you must visit the Whale Museum. The museum is involved in all whale-related activities in the San Juan Islands, sponsoring laboratory and field research, educational programs, workshops, and whale-watching trips. Open year-round; call for hours. Nominal admission fee.

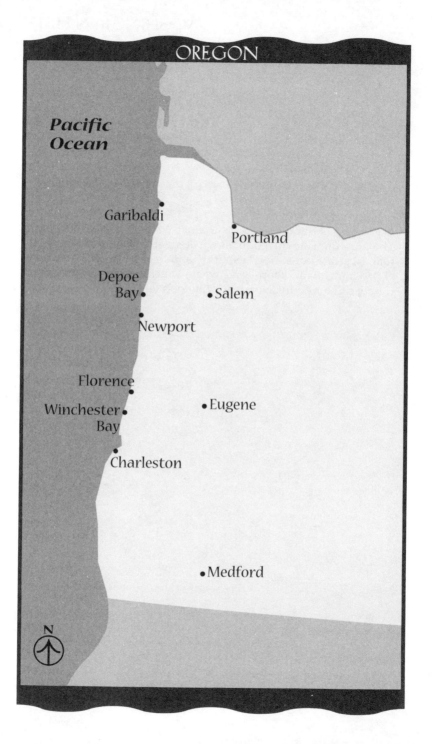

7

OREGON

Whether you prefer to stand on the shore or venture out on a boat, you'll find excellent whale watching along Oregon's spectacular 400-mile-long coastline. Onshore whale watching is better organized here than anywhere else in the United States, at least during the two annual state-sponsored Whale Watching Weeks, which are held during the peak periods of the northward and southward gray whale migrations. From the day after Christmas through New Year's Day and for one week in March, volunteers staff nearly 20 sites along the Oregon shoreline for several hours each day to offer information and assistance to whale watchers. Just look for the signs that declare: "Whale Watching Spoken Here."

A resident population of about 200 gray whales has been summering off the Oregon coast in recent years, which means there's year-round whale watching near several ports. Harbor porpoises are common here, although Dall's porpoises are much less common. Harbor seals and California and Steller's sea lions are fairly common.

The cancellation of the salmon fishing season for two years running has put many charter fishing operators out of business, some of whom offered whale-watching tours during the gray whale migrations. Several charter boats now take people out whale watching after returning from their early morning fishing trips. Others are dedicated entirely to whale-watching and natural history cruises. Rough seas and winter weather off the Oregon coast can keep the whale-watching fleet in port, so call ahead to be sure the boats are sailing.

Garibaldi

During the spring migration, gray whales are often seen just outside the Tillamook Bay jetties. In recent years some gray whales have been summer residents at the nearby Three-Arches National Wildlife Refuge, but they are not easily approached. Sea lions, seals, and marine birds are also found at Three-Arches. Harbor porpoises are common, and Pacific white-sided dolphins are becoming more common. Dall's porpoises and orcas are rarely sighted.

Depoe Bay

Depoe Bay bills itself as both "The World's Smallest Harbor" and "The Whale Watching Capital of the Oregon Coast," which it very well may be, receiving more than 50,000 whale watchers a year. The town has good facilities for visitors, and accommodation/whale-watching packages are available.

Gray whales are in the Depoe Bay area almost year-round. Their southward and northward migrations run from November through May, and there's a resident population in the summer. In addition, sightings of orcas (usually in April and May) and humpbacks are occasionally reported. Harbor seals, and California and Steller's sea lions are commonly seen. Dall's porpoises are rarely spotted, and Pacific white-sided dolphins are seen occasionally.

Newport

Just down the coast from Depoe Bay, Newport is the proud home of the Oregon Coast Aquarium and the Mark O. Hatfield Marine Science Center of Oregon State University. Both institutions have extensive education and research programs, and any whale watcher will find them worth a visit. An active fishing center, the town has several experienced whale-watching operators. Departure times from Newport are dependent on the tides, since navigating the harbor mouth bar can be very tricky.

Winchester Bay

Winchester Bay boasts a beautiful, unspoiled harbor that receives very little tourist traffic. Across the street from the Umpqua Lighthouse, a whale-watching platform is perched on the bluffs overlooking the Pacific.

1. Observation platform on Columbia River south jetty in Fort Stevens State Park, west of Astoria, two miles off Highway 101.
2. Tillamook Head, Ecola State Park.
3. Cape Falcon, Oswald West State Park.
4. Neahkahnie Mountain, Oswald West State Park.
5. Cape Meares.
6. Three Capes Scenic Route.
7. Cape Lookout.
8. Cape Kiwanda.
9. Cascade Head, Siuslaw National Forest.
10. Depoe Bay.
11. Cape Foulweather.
12. Yaquina Head, Agate Beach.
13. Cape Perpetua.
14. Heceta Head.
15. Umpqua Lighthouse.
16. Sea Lion Caves.
17. Cape Arago State Park.
18. Cape Blanco State Park.
19. Highway 101, south of Port Orford to Gold Beach.
20. Humbug Mountain State Park.
21. Cape Sebastian State Park.
22. Samuel H. Boardman State Park.
23. Harris Beach State Park.

Garibaldi Tour Operators

Garibaldi/D&D Charters

Seventh Street at Highway 101
P.O. Box 556
Garibaldi, OR 97118
503/322–0381, 800/900–4665

Captain: Doug Davis.
Season: March and April; Christmas/New Year's season.
Boats: Three 38-foot fishing boats, 15 passengers each.
Times: Two-hour trip daily at 11 A.M.
Cost: $15 per person.
Departs: Garibaldi Harbor.
Refreshments: Beverages.
Miscellaneous: In business since 1983. Captain narrates.

Siggi-G Charters

P.O. Box 536
Garibaldi, OR 97118
503/322–3285

Captain: Joe Ockensels.
Season: March and April.
Boat: *Siggi-G,* a 40-foot charter fishing boat, 15 passengers.
Times: Two-hour trip daily, usually in the early afternoon, depending on tides.
Cost: $20 per person.
Departs: Garibaldi Boat Basin.
Refreshments: Coffee.
Miscellaneous: In the whale-watching business for more than 10 years. Experienced skipper narrates. Wheelchairs accommodated.

Troller Deep Sea Fishing Charters

P.O. Box 452
604 Mooring Basin Road
Garibaldi, OR 97118
503/322–3666, 503/322–3796

Owner: Lawrence S. Vandecoevering.
Season: March to mid-May.
Boats: Three 37- to 50-foot boats, 19 to 28 passengers.
Times: Two- to two-and-a-half-hour trips daily, depending on tides and demand.
Cost: $15 per person; children under 12 are two for one.
Departs: Garibaldi Boat Basin.
Refreshments: Coffee and water.
Miscellaneous: In business since 1957, with a long history of offering whale- and bird-watching trips. Experienced crew narrates.

Depoe Bay Tour Operators

Dockside Charters

P.O. Box 1308
270 Southeast Coast Guard Place
Depoe Bay, OR 97341
503/765–2545, 800/733–8915

Season: Year-round, weather permitting.
Boats: A 43-foot boat and a 45-foot boat, 30 passengers each.
Times: One-hour trips daily (one and a half hours during gray whale migration); call for times.
Cost: $9 an hour per person; $6 an hour for children 4 to 12; children under 4 free.

Departs: Depoe Bay Harbor.
Refreshments: Coffee provided.
Miscellaneous: In the whale-watching business since 1982.

Tradewinds Charters

P.O. Box 123
Depoe Bay, OR 97341
503/765–2345, 800/676–7819

Owner: Rich Allyn.
Season: Year-round.
Boats: Fleet of 12 vessels; 6 to 42 passengers.
Times: Two-and-a-half-hour whale-watching cruises (call for schedule).
Cost: $20 per person, children 5 and under free.
Departs: Depoe Bay Harbor.
Refreshments: Bring your own.
Miscellaneous: In operation since 1990. Wheelchairs accommodated.

Newport Tour Operators

Marine Discovery Tours

345 SW Bay Boulevard
Newport, OR 97365
503/265–6200, 800/903–2628

Owners: Don and Fran Mathews.
Season: Year-round.
Boat: *Discovery*, a 65-foot custom-built whale-watching and marine education vessel, 49 passengers.
Times: Two-hour trip on weekdays at 1 P.M., and on weekends at 11 A.M. and 1:30 P.M.
Cost: $16 per person; $8 for children 5 to 12; children under 5 free.
Departs: Newport's Historic Bay Front.
Refreshments: Coffee.
Miscellaneous: In 1994, after 12 seasons as commercial fishers in the Bering Sea, the Mathews founded Marine Discovery Tours, a whale-watching/marine wildlife education operation. According to Christy Layton, their full-time marine educator, *Discovery* was designed to be a floating classroom, complete with two 32-inch television monitors.

Newport Sportfishing

1000 SE Bay Boulevard
Newport, OR 97365
503/265–7558, 800/828–8777

Owners: John and Roz Vostinak.
Season: Year-round, weather permitting.
Boats: Fleet of 40- to 50-foot sportfishermen, 6 to 26 passengers.
Times: Two- to two-and-a-half-hour trips daily around 1 P.M.
Cost: $15 per person; $7.50 for children 7 to 12; children under 7 free.
Departs: Embarcadero Marina, Bay Boulevard, Newport.
Refreshments: Coffee.
Miscellaneous: Newport Sportfishing has over 10 years' experience offering whale-watching tours. The Vostinaks have owned the business since 1993. Experienced captains narrate.

Newport Tradewinds

653 SW Bay Boulevard
Newport, OR 97365
503/265–2101, 800/676–7819

Owner: Bert Waddell.
Season: April to November.
Boats: Nine charter fishing boats, 38 to 56 feet, 18 to 44 passengers.
Times: Depends on demand and tides.
Cost: $20 per person; children under six free.
Departs: Newport Harbor.
Refreshments: Coffee.
Miscellaneous: Offering whale-watching trips since 1971. Experienced captains and crew narrate. Wheelchairs accommodated.

Sea Gull Charters

343 SW Bay Boulevard
Newport, OR 97365
503/265–7441, 800/865–7441

Owner: Dick Overfield.
Season: Year-round.
Boats: *Battlecry*, a 50-foot ocean racing sloop, 6 passengers; five motorized charter fishing boats, 30 to 62 feet, 6 to 50 passengers.
Times: *Battlecry* (two and a half hours) daily at 10 A.M. and 1 P.M. (plus 4 P.M. and 7 P.M. in the summer); motor fleet (two hours) daily at 10:30 A.M. and 1:30 P.M.

Cost: $30 per person for *Battlecry;* $16 per person for motor fleet; half-price for children under 13.
Departs: Newport Harbor.
Refreshments: Coffee.
Miscellaneous: Over 10 years' whale-watching experience. Skippers narrate. Wheelchairs accommodated.

Florence Tour Operator

Siuslaw Charters

P.O. Box 2399
Florence, OR 97439
503/997–9049, 800/997–8961

Owner: Dan Owens.
Captain: Barry Burks.
Season: Year-round.
Boat: *Kenny Boy,* a 42-foot fishing boat, 20 passengers.
Times: Two-and-a-half- to three-hour trip every morning.
Cost: $25 per person; $15 for children under 12.
Departs: Old Town Harbor, Florence.
Refreshments: Coffee.
Miscellaneous: In the whale-watching business since 1993. Captain Burks is a trained naturalist. Wheelchairs accommodated.

Winchester Bay Tour Operator

Gee Gee Charters, Inc.

465 Beach Boulevard
Winchester Bay, OR 97467
503/271–3152

Captains: Gilbert and Scott Howard.
Season: December to May.
Boats: *Gee Gee,* a 48-foot charter boat, 20 passengers; *Lit'l Gee,* a 34-foot sportfisherman, 8 passengers.
Times: One- to three-hour trips, per demand.
Cost: $10 an hour per person.
Departs: Winchester Harbor.
Refreshments: Bring your own.
Miscellaneous: A family-owned business for more than 35 years; offering whale-watching trips since 1993. Wheelchairs accommodated.

Charleston/South Beach Tour Operator

Betty Kay Charters

P.O. Box 5020
Charleston, OR 97420
503/888–9021, 800/752–6303

Captain: Bill Whitmer.
Season: November to May; year-round when whales are in the area.
Boat: *Betty Kay,* a 50-foot sportfisher, 35 passengers.
Times: Two- to three-hour trips, depending on tides and demand.
Cost: $15 per person; children under six free.
Departs: Charleston Boat Basin.
Refreshments: Coffee. Bring your own snacks.
Miscellaneous: Wheelchairs accommodated.

RESOURCES

Depoe Bay Chamber of Commerce

P.O. Box 21
630 Highway 101
Depoe Bay, OR 97341
503/765–2889

Greater Newport Chamber of Commerce

555 SW Coast Highway
Newport, OR 97365
503/265–8801, 800/262–7844

Mark O. Hatfield Marine Science Center

Oregon State University
2030 South Marine Science Drive
Newport, OR 97365
503/867–0100

This active research and teaching facility draws half a million visitors yearly. The Hatfield Center trains the hundreds of volunteers who staff the coastal lookouts during the two annual Oregon Coast Whale Watching Weeks. World-famous cetologist Dr. Bruce Mate is on the faculty, and visitors are sometimes treated to a demonstration of his pioneering work in radiotelemetric whale tagging. Whales as far away as the Bay of Fundy on Canada's Atlantic coast are tagged with miniaturized radio transmitters that record location, movement, and diving behavior. This information is transmitted via satellite to Dr. Mate's lab in Newport, where researchers receive the data in real time. It might read: "Right whale #56 just surfaced after a 32-minute dive to a maximum depth of 550 feet and is now 300 miles off the coast of Nova Scotia and heading southeast at a speed of 3 knots." Open daily; call for hours. Admission is free.

The Oregon Coast Aquarium

2820 SE Ferry Slip Road
Newport, OR 97365
503/867–3474

This state-of-the-art aquarium opened in 1992 and offers a number of exhibits focusing on the ecology of the Oregon Coast. Seals, sea otters, and sea lions live in outdoor habitats. Indoors, there are permanent and changing exhibits of other animals. A film on gray whales is screened frequently. Open daily; call for hours. Admission fee.

Sea Lion Caves

91560 Highway 101
Florence, OR 97439
503/547–3111

The only mainland site for viewing wild Steller's sea lions year-round is located just 11 miles north of Florence. A stairway and an elevator take you 206 feet down to a 1,500-foot-long sea cave where you can observe the sea lions up close. Open daily, but call ahead for specific hours. Admission fee.

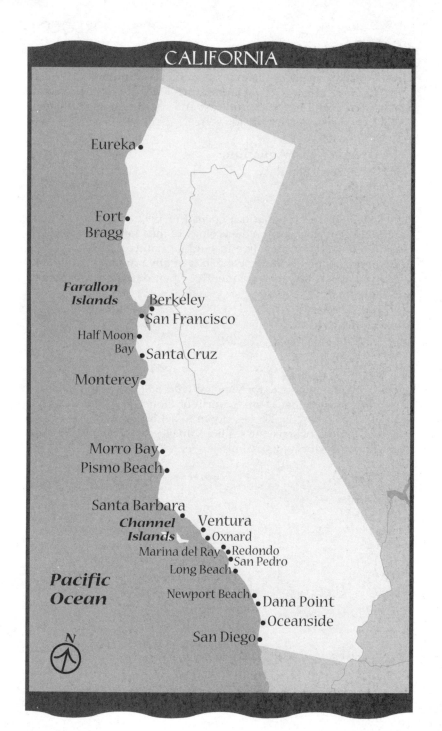

CALIFORNIA

Eureka

Fort
Bragg

*Farallon
Islands*   Berkeley
           San Francisco
Half Moon
Bay   Santa Cruz

Monterey

Morro Bay
Pismo Beach

Santa Barbara
Channel   Ventura
Islands   Oxnard
          Marina del Ray Redondo
                          San Pedro
               Long Beach

*Pacific
Ocean*

               Newport Beach Dana Point
                              Oceanside
               San Diego

N

8

CALIFORNIA

Every year, more people watch whales off California's thousand-mile-long coastline than in any other region in the world. And while the overwhelming majority come out to see the gray whale migrations in winter and spring, the state does offer a wide range of alternative opportunities for viewing whales and other marine mammals. In recent years, humpback and blue whales have been spotted regularly during the summer and fall in the Channel Islands, Monterey Bay, and the Farallon Islands near San Francisco. Dolphins and porpoises are common in many areas, as are seals, sea lions, and elephant seals. Sea otters are established residents from Big Sur up to Santa Cruz, and to see them happily floating in their natural habitat all you have to do is stroll along Cannery Row in Monterey.

Whale watching in California needn't be a day- or weeklong affair. If you are strapped for time and cash you can take a two-hour, $12 jaunt with an operator who guarantees a whale sighting or your money back. And for landlubbers, gray whales can be spotted from literally hundreds of locations along the coast.

One thing to remember: California whale watching takes place on the open Pacific, so be prepared for cool temperatures and a rolling ocean swell.

NORTH COAST

Eureka and Fort Bragg

Nearly all the whale-watching activity in the northern part of the state is centered around the northward gray whale migration in the spring. Two communities on the north coast sponsor annual whale-watching celebrations. There's the Mendocino Whale Festival in early March and the Fort Bragg Whale Festival in mid-March. During these times, the small towns are packed with visitors, and Fort Bragg charter boats are continually taking people out whale watching. Tour operators enlist the help of extra boats, in addition to those mentioned in this chapter.

San Francisco Bay Area

Aside from the occasional gray or humpback that wanders in, gets lost in the Sacramento River or near Petaluma, and becomes a media celebrity, there isn't much in the way of whale watching inside San Francisco Bay.

San Francisco Bay *is* a prime location for viewing pinnipeds, however. Seals and sea lions can be seen anywhere in the bay, especially during herring runs. The city of Sausalito has a waterfront graced with its trademark sea lion sculpture . . . and the real thing. Sea lions frequent the downtown area of upscale Tiburon. Several harbor seal breeding grounds are in the area: Coyote Point in the South Bay, and Bolinas Lagoon, Tomales Bay, and Point Reyes in the North Bay.

Several years ago an enterprising sea lion abandoned his wave-battered post on Seal Rock outside San Francisco's Golden Gate and sought the snug harbor of the Pier 39 Marina. Word spread quickly among his pals, and the entire sea lion complement shifted its quarters permanently, displacing yachts and overrunning the docks. The sea lions are now a major tourist attraction and educational showcase, courtesy of the Marine Mammal Center's interpretive tours. Just stop by Pier 39, or call 415/289–7330 for information on tours and programs.

Outside the Golden Gate and up along the Marin and Point Reyes coastlines, gray whales are spotted frequently during their winter and spring migrations. Harbor porpoises are seen frequently near the mouth of the Gate.

Just 26 miles west of San Francisco's Golden Gate, eight rocky islands jut up from the sea: the Farallones. These isolated granite outcroppings, barren and forbidding, look from a distance about as capable of sustaining life as the surface of the moon. But they are home to one of the richest and most diverse treasures of marine life in the hemisphere. The wealth of fauna results from nutrient-rich currents welling up from the nearby edge of the continental shelf, supporting a food chain that ranges from tiny plankton to huge blue whales.

The islands are a tightly guarded nature preserve, and only a handful of researchers are allowed to land here at any given time. However, natural history day cruises to Southeast Farallon Island are offered from summer through fall, and passengers get close enough to see the incredible profusion of marine mammals and birds.

Southeast Farallon Island is a regular habitat for five species of pinnipeds: California sea lions, Steller's sea lions, Northern elephant seals, harbor seals, and Northern fur seals. Rare visits from a solitary Guadalupe fur seal have been recorded. Virtually every square foot of beach space is occupied, and sea lions even perch high on the island's granite slopes. When the sea lion chorus begins (or when the island's thousands of seabirds are present), the din is deafening. Young sea lions surf the incoming waves or use huge elephant seals as blubbery mattresses. Harbor seals drape themselves over low rocks. And lurking offshore in the cold waters are great white sharks, eager for another seal meal.

The waters of the surrounding Gulf of the Farallones provide some of California's best summer and fall whale watching. Humpback and blue whales have been appearing regularly in recent years, and one or both species is spotted on most trips. They come to these nutrient-rich waters to feed on the masses of tiny shrimplike krill in May and stay through October or November.

But there may be a price to be paid to get close to all this marine life: the seas around the Farallones are on average as rough and unfriendly to weak stomachs as any whale-watching waters in the world.

Half Moon Bay

Just down the coast from San Francisco and home to the now world-famous surfing break at Mavericks, which claimed the life of renowned big-wave surfer Mark Foo in 1994, Princeton Harbor at Half Moon Bay is home to an active charter fishing fleet that takes thousands of whale watchers out during the gray whale migration.

Santa Cruz

This beach and university town at the northern end of Monterey Bay offers an interesting range of whale-watching and natural history trips. Seals, sea lions, and occasional sea otters can be easily seen from shore. A group of "pier bum" sea lions hangs out on the pilings below the end of the municipal pier.

Monterey Bay

The waters in and around Monterey Bay offer an astounding variety of marine life. A deepwater submarine canyon comes right into the bay, ending just offshore near Moss Landing. The canyon's unique size, shape, and proximity to the shore, combined with a strong seasonal upwelling of nutrient-rich waters, produce an extremely fertile marine ecosystem, including both warm- and cold-water species. Marine algae, fish, birds, and mammals thrive here.

The annual gray whale migration is a major event in the area, when dozens of boat operators and innkeepers team up to provide whale-watching packages. The grays favor the city of Monterey, passing close to Point Pinos and Cypress Point on their southbound and northbound migrations; many whales take a looping detour right into the bay near Monterey's wharf area. During the summer months, humpbacks and blues are regularly spotted offshore on whale-watching trips. Pacific white-sided dolphins and Dall's porpoises are seen year-round.

The entire Monterey Peninsula offers myriad chances to view seals, sea lions, and sea otters, from the cliffs of Point Lobos south of Carmel to the promenade along Cannery Row. Observation spots downtown include the Coast Guard and Municipal piers and Fisherman's Wharf, and farther out of town there's Lover's Point, Otter Point, Point Pinos, Point Joe, Cypress Point, Pescadero Point, Point Lobos, and Garrapata State Park. Virtually all of the suitable offshore rocks and kelp beds are frequented by some enterprising marine mammal.

One of the best and most accessible ways in the world to view sea otters is at the Monterey Bay Aquarium. In addition to a sea otter tank, this extremely popular facility has an outside lagoon where orphaned otter pups receive swimming and grooming lessons from their human surrogate moms before being returned to the wild.

CENTRAL COAST

Morro Bay

Down the coast from Big Sur, Morro Bay is a commercial fishing port. Nearby Hearst Castle draws hundreds of thousands of visitors to the area each year.

Channel Islands and Santa Barbara

The Channel Islands, located approximately 20 miles off the Santa Barbara coast, were declared a National Marine Sanctuary in 1980. The sanctuary, which includes five of the eight Channel Islands—Santa Rosa, Anacapa, Santa Cruz, Santa Barbara, and San Miguel—is home to sea otters and six species of pinnipeds. More than 27 species of whales and dolphins, including blue, gray, humpback, and sei whales, are found at one time or another in the waters surrounding the islands. Thousands of seals and sea lions haul out to breed and bask in the sun. Sea otters anchor out amid tangled kelp beds to groom and feed. Call 805/642–1393 for information on day trips, extended visits, seasonal sightings, and special tours.

SOUTH COAST

The annual gray whale migration is the prime focus of whale-watching operators in southern California. Other species are seen only sporadically, since most of the boats don't venture out farther than necessary to spot grays. Because southern California's beaches are so heavily trafficked by humans throughout the year, and because there aren't many offshore islands, most seals and sea lions have moved to other habitats, making them more difficult to find than elsewhere in the state. Seals and sea lions will usually haul out on a "human" beach only if they are sick or injured.

Pinnipeds, however, can be seen off La Jolla, Carpinteria, and Ventura, cruising along the surf line in search of a meal, perched on an offshore reef at low tide, or checking out the surfer scene.

ONSHORE WHALE-WATCHING SITES IN CALIFORNIA

Del Norte County

1. Point Saint George, five miles north of Crescent City.
2. Crescent Beach Overlook, a half-mile south of Crescent City.
3. Crescent Beach in Redwood National Park, four miles south of Crescent City.
4. Prairie Creek Redwoods State Park, seven miles north of Orick.

Humboldt County

1. Redwood National Park, in Orick.
2. Patricks Point State Park, between Orick and Eureka.
3. Vista Point, 14 miles north of Eureka.
4. Trinidad Head, Trinidad State Beach, just south of Patricks Point.
5. Clam Beach, 12 miles north of Eureka.

Mendocino County

Coastal overlooks are located along the entire length of Highway 1 in Mendocino County.

1. MacKerricher State Park, three miles north of Fort Bragg, particularly Laguna Point.
2. Todd's Point, just south of Noyo Harbor Bridge on Ocean View Drive, Fort Bragg.
3. Jughandle State Reserve and Caspar Headlands State Beach & Recreation Area, five miles south of Fort Bragg.
4. Russian Gulch State Park, three miles north of Mendocino.
5. Mendocino Headlands State Park, outside the town of Mendocino.
6. Manchester State Beach Park, 30 miles south of Mendocino.
7. Point Arena Lighthouse, three miles north of the town of Point Arena.
8. Gualala Point in Gualala Point County Park, at Mendocino/Sonoma county line, 110 miles north of San Francisco.

Sonoma County

Coastal overlooks are located along the entire length of Highway 1 in Sonoma County.

1. Salt Point in Salt Point State Park, 20 miles north of Jenner.
2. Stillwater Cove County Park, three miles north of Fort Ross.
3. Fort Ross State Historic Park, 10 miles north of Jenner.
4. Sonoma Coast State Beach, just south of Jenner.
5. Bodega Head, four miles west of the town of Bodega Bay.

ONSHORE WHALE-WATCHING SITES IN CALIFORNIA

Marin County

1. Point Reyes National Seashore, including Point Reyes Lighthouse at the tip of the Point Reyes Peninsula (best in early January), Chimney Rock (mid-March), and Tomales Point (May). Call the visitors center at the Point Reyes Lighthouse, 415/669–1534, for schedules and reservations for naturalist-guided whale-watching seminars and tours. About 1 ½ hours north of the Golden Gate Bridge.

San Francisco County

1. The Cliff House, Ocean Beach, San Francisco.

San Mateo County

1. Gray Whale Cove State Beach, Devil's Slide, 12 miles south of the Cliff House.
2. Montara State Beach, two miles south of Gray Whale Cove.
3. Half Moon Bay State Beach, Half Moon Bay.
4. San Gregorio State Beach (from the cliffs north and south of the main beach parking area), 11 miles south of Half Moon Bay.
5. Pebble Beach and Bean Hollow state beaches, 16 miles south of Half Moon Bay.
6. Pigeon Point Lighthouse, seven miles north of Año Nuevo.
7. Año Nuevo State Reserve, 20 miles north of Santa Cruz.

Santa Cruz County

1. Greyhound Rock, 19 miles north of Santa Cruz.
2. Davenport Landing, a former coastal whaling station, 14 miles north of Santa Cruz.

Monterey County

1. Point Pinos, Pacific Grove, just south of Monterey.
2. Point Lobos State Reserve, just south of Carmel. Highway lookouts south to Point Sur.
3. Garrapata State Park, seven miles south of Carmel.
4. Bixby Creek Bridge, at the northern end of Big Sur.
5. Point Sur State Historic Park, Big Sur, 18 miles south of Carmel.
6. Julia Pfeiffer Burns State Park, Los Padres National Forest, 37 miles south of Carmel. Rangers lead whale programs on weekends in January and February.

San Luis Obispo County

1. Ragged Point, at the southern end of Big Sur, five miles north of Hearst San Simeon State Historical Monument.
2. San Simeon State Beach, five miles south of San Simeon.
3. Moonstone Beach Drive Lookout and Leffingwell Landing in Cambria, eight miles south of San Simeon.
4. Cayucos State Beach, 10 miles north of Morro Bay.
5. Morro Bay State Park, Morro Bay.
6. Montaño de Oro State Park, 10 miles south of Morro Bay.

Santa Barbara County

1. Point Sal, Point Sal State Beach, 10 miles west of Guadalupe.
2. Gaviota State Beach, 26 miles north of Santa Barbara.
3. Goleta State Beach, two miles north of Santa Barbara.
4. Arroyo Burro Beach County Park and Shoreline Park, in the city of Santa Barbara.

Ventura County

1. Pitas Point, six miles north of Ventura.
2. Ventura, lookout tower on Spinnaker Drive.
3. Anacapa Island, reached via ferry from Ventura.
4. Point Mugu Rock and Point Mugu State Park, 12 miles south of Ventura.
5. Lookouts along Highway 1 south of Point Mugu to Los Angeles County line.

Los Angeles County

1. Highway 1 south from the county line along the Malibu coast, including Leo Carrillo State Park, at the county line, and Point Dume State Beach bluffs, seven miles north of Malibu.
2. Point Vicente County Park, 31501 Palos Verdes Drive West in Palos Verdes. Site of the Point Vicente Interpretive Center, which has whale-watching materials, programs, and a viewing center.
3. Point Fermin Park and Lighthouse, San Pedro, near Los Angeles Harbor.
4. White Point at Royal Palms State Beach, San Pedro.

Orange County

1. Corona Del Mar State Beach, bluffs south of Newport Beach.
2. Laguna Beach Vista Point, Laguna Beach.
3. Blue Lantern Lookout Park, Dana Point, eight miles south of Laguna Beach.

San Diego County

1. Bluffs along Interstate 5 from San Clemente to Oceanside.
2. San Onofre State Beach, two miles south of San Onofre.
3. Bluffs along Highway 1, from Encinitas to Del Mar.
4. Torrey Pines State Beach and Reserve, five miles north of La Jolla.
5. Point La Jolla, and along ocean viewpoints in La Jolla.
6. Cabrillo National Monument, Point Loma, San Diego County. Whale-watching station with an observatory.

NORTH COAST TOUR OPERATORS

Eureka, Fort Bragg, and Mendocino Tour Operators

Anchor Charters

P.O. Box 103
Fort Bragg, CA 95437
707/964–3854, 707/964–4550

Owner: Rick Thornton
Season: December 26 to mid-April.
Boats: *Trek II*, 56 feet, 49 passengers; *Cavalier*, 50 feet, 22 passengers; *Lady Irma II*, 45 feet, 22 passengers.
Times: Two-hour cruises depart Monday to Friday at 11 A.M. and 1 P.M., and Saturday and Sunday at 8 A.M., 10 A.M., noon, and 2 P.M.
Cost: $20 per person; $14 for children 5 to 12; children under 5 free.
Departs: Noyo Harbor in Fort Bragg.
Refreshments: Snack bar.
Miscellaneous: Busiest during the Fort Bragg Whale Festival.

Coast Flyers, Inc.

43001 Little River Airport Road
Little River, CA 95456
707/937–1224

Owner: John Merriman.
Season: Late November to April.
Craft: Cessna 172 single-engine airplane.
Times: Call for reservation.

Cost: $75 minimum (total) for one to three passengers for a half-hour; $115 an hour.
Departs: Little River Airport.
Miscellaneous: Get a unique bird's-eye view of the gray whale migration from a small plane.

King Salmon Charters

3458 Utah Street
Eureka, CA 95503
707/442–3474

Captain: Dennis Pecaut.
Season: February to April.
Boat: *The Moku,* a 36-foot sportfisherman, six passengers.
Times: One-and-a-half- to two-hour private charter cruises; call for reservations.
Cost: $50 an hour per person.
Departs: King Salmon Resort in Humboldt Bay.
Refreshments: Coffee.
Miscellaneous: Captain Pecaut takes small groups on whale-watching cruises. Whales pass within three or four miles of the shore.

Misty II Charters

P.O. Box 223
Fort Bragg, CA 95437
707/964–7161

Owners: Charlie and Peggy Johnson.
Season: February and March.
Boat: *Misty II,* a 44-foot sportfisherman, 26 passengers.
Times: Two-hour trip daily; call for times.
Cost: $20 per person.
Departs: Noyo Harbor in Fort Bragg.
Refreshments: Coffee.
Miscellaneous: Busiest during the Fort Bragg and Mendocino whale festivals.

San Francisco Bay Area Tour Operators

Dolphin Charters

1007 Leneve Place
El Cerrito, CA 94530
510/527–9622

Captain: Ronn Storro-Patterson.
Season: Farallon Islands—April, October, and November; gray whale migration—January to May.

Boat: M. V. *Delphinus,* a 50-foot motor yacht designed for natural history cruises, 40 passengers.

Times: Farallon Islands—weekends from 7 A.M. to 6 P.M.; gray whale migration—weekends from 7 A.M. to 6 P.M. and sometimes 9 A.M. to 1 P.M. Extra seats are often available on weekday group charters. Call for times and reservations for all trips.

Cost: $69 per person full day; $49 per person half-day; half-price for children under 18 (must be accompanied by an adult).

Departs: Berkeley Marina.

Refreshments: Galley has beverages and hot food.

Miscellaneous: Captain Ronn Storro-Patterson is a professional biologist and a former university professor. Dolphin Charters specializes in natural history cruises and education. On half-day whale-watching trips, boats stay near the shoreline and avoid the rougher outer waters.

Oceanic Society Expeditions

Fort Mason Center, Building E
San Francisco, CA 94123
415/474–3385

Season: Farallon Islands—June to November; Gray whale migration—late December to April.

Boat: *New Superfish,* a 63-foot motor vessel, 48 passengers.

Times: Farallon Islands—weekends and selected Fridays and Mondays from 8:30 A.M. to 5 P.M.; gray whale migration—weekends and selected Fridays and Mondays from 9:30 A.M. to 4:30 P.M.

Cost: Farallon Islands—$58 per person on Saturday and Sunday, $49 on Friday and Monday; gray whale migration—$48 per person on Saturday and Sunday, $45 on Friday and Monday.

Departs: San Francisco Yacht Harbor.

Refreshments: Bring your own snacks and beverages.

Miscellaneous: Oceanic Society naturalists accompany all cruises. Farallon Islands trips offer an extraordinary variety of marine life. Children under 10 are not permitted, and children under 15 must be accompanied by an adult.

Half Moon Bay Tour Operators

Captain John's Sportfishing

P.O. Box 155
Half Moon Bay, CA 94019
415/726–2913, 415/728–3377

Owner: John Teixeira.

Season: Mid-December to early May.

Boat: *The Outlaw,* a 55-foot charter boat, 40 passengers.

Times: Two-and-a-half-hour cruises on weekends at 10 A.M. and 1 P.M.
Cost: $20 per person; $15 for children under 13.
Departs: Pillar Point Harbor in Half Moon Bay.
Refreshments: Hot drinks on board; food available at the harbor.
Miscellaneous: The experienced captain narrates.

Huck Finn's Sportfishing

P.O. Box 1432
El Granada, CA 94018
415/726–7133

Owners: Bill and Peggy Becket.
Season: January to April, depending on the whales.
Boats: Three 43- to 54-foot sportfishing boats, 22 to 46 passengers.
Times: Two-and-a-half- to three-hour trips on the weekends at 10 A.M. and 1:30 P.M.
Cost: $18 per person; $15 for children under 13.
Departs: Pillar Point Harbor in Half Moon Bay.
Refreshments: Snacks sold at the harbor.
Miscellaneous: Narration by experienced skippers.

Oceanic Society Expeditions

Fort Mason Center, Building E
San Francisco, CA 94123
415/474–3385

Season: Late December to April.
Boat: *Salty Lady*, 56 feet, 48 passengers.
Times: Three-hour cruises on weekends and selected Fridays and Mondays at 9 A.M. and 1 P.M.
Cost: Saturday and Sunday—$32 per person, $30 for seniors (60 and up) and children 5 to 15; Fridays—$29 per person, $27 for seniors and children.
Departs: Pillar Point Harbor in Half Moon Bay.
Refreshments: Hot drinks on board; food available at the harbor.
Miscellaneous: Oceanic Society naturalists accompany all trips.

Santa Cruz Tour Operators

Chardonnay II

P.O. Box 66966
Scotts Valley, CA 95067–6966
408/423–1213

Season: Early February to mid-October.
Boat: *Chardonnay II*, 70-foot racing/sailing yacht, 49 passengers.
Times: Two- to three-hour cruises; call for times.

Cost: $35 per person.
Departs: Santa Cruz Harbor.
Refreshments: Galley on board; some refreshments included.
Miscellaneous: Go whale watching aboard a high-tech "super yacht" that has won open-ocean races. Some cruises are narrated by docents from UC Santa Cruz's Long Marine Laboratory.

Stagnaro Fishing Trips

P.O. Box 1340
Santa Cruz, CA 95061
408/427–2334, 408/423–2010

Owners: The Stagnaro family.
Season: Mid-December to mid-April.
Boat: *Stagnaro II*, a 65-foot charter boat, 60 passengers.
Times: Two-and-a-half-hour trips daily per demand.
Cost: $16 per person; $12 for children under 14.
Departs: Santa Cruz Wharf and Santa Cruz Harbor.
Refreshments: Snack bar.
Miscellaneous: Captain and crew narrate.

Monterey Bay Tour Operators

Chris' Sportfishing

48 Fisherman's Wharf
Monterey, CA 93940
408/375–5951

Season: December 26 to mid-March.
Boats: Four 55- to 70-foot boats, 40 to 74 passengers.
Times: Two-hour cruises daily; call for times.
Cost: $12 per person; $6 for children under 13.
Departs: Fisherman's Wharf, Monterey Harbor.
Refreshments: Food available at the wharf.
Miscellaneous: Experienced crew narrates.

Monterey Sport Fishing and Cruises

96 Old Fisherman's Wharf #1
Monterey, CA 93940
408/372–2203

Owner: The Shake family.
Season: Mid-December to mid-March, June to October.
Boats: Three 50- to 75-foot boats, 45 to 100 passengers.
Times: One-and-a-half- to two-hour trips in the winter depart hourly on the weekends from 9 A.M. to 3 P.M. and on weekdays at 9 A.M., noon, and 3 P.M. Three-hour trips daily in the summer, call for schedule.

Cost: Winter—$14 per person, $8 for children under 12; summer—$25 per person, $20 for children.

Departs: Old Fisherman's Wharf, Monterey Harbor.

Refreshments: Galley on board the largest boat only. Bring your own food and drinks for the others.

Miscellaneous: American Cetacean Society members narrate on weekends, and experienced captains and crew narrate during the week.

Oceanic Society Expeditions

Fort Mason Center, Building E
San Francisco, CA 94123
415/441–1106, 800/326–7491

Season: August to October.

Boat: M. V. *Point Sur Clipper*, a 55-foot research vessel, 12 passengers.

Times: Seven-day Monterey Bay dolphin and whale research cruises depart weekly; daylong working research cruises return to land each night; call for times.

Cost: $590 per person; meals and lodging not included.

Departs: Fisherman's Wharf, Monterey Harbor.

Miscellaneous: This is a serious research program surveying the marine mammal resources of Monterey Bay, particularly Pacific white-sided dolphins and humpback whales. Oceanic Society naturalists and sponsored research scientists accompany all trips. Participants are part of the research team.

Randy's Sportfishing

66 Fisherman's Wharf
Monterey, CA 93940
408/372–7440

Owner: Peter Bruno.

Season: Mid-December to March.

Boats: Three 53- to 65-foot boats, 48 to 68 passengers.

Times: Two-hour trips on weekdays at 10:30 A.M., 12:30 P.M., and 2:30 P.M., and hourly on weekends from 9:30 A.M. to 2:30 P.M.

Cost: $14 per person; $10 for children under 13.

Departs: Fisherman's Wharf, Monterey Harbor.

Refreshments: Food available at the wharf.

Miscellaneous: Randy's has offered whale-watching cruises for almost 30 years. Experienced skippers narrate on weekdays, and most weekend trips are narrated by naturalists and/or marine biologists from the Monterey Bay Aquarium.

Sam's Fishing

84 Fisherman's Wharf #1
Monterey, CA 93940
408/372–0577

Owner: Fred Montford.
Season: January to mid-March.
Boats: Three 55- to 65-foot sportfishing boats, 44 to 60 passengers.
Times: Two-hour cruises on weekends at 9 A.M., 11 A.M., 1 P.M., and 3 P.M.; call for reservations and weekday times.
Cost: $12 per person; $8 for children under 13.
Departs: Fisherman's Wharf, Monterey Harbor.
Refreshments: Food available at the wharf.
Miscellaneous: Experienced captains provide commentary.

Shearwater Journeys

P.O. Box 1445
Soquel, CA 95073
408/688–1990

Owner: Debra Love Shearwater.
Season: Mid-January to mid-February for gray whales; year-round for seabirds and marine mammals.
Boats: Three 55- to 65-foot sportfishing boats, 44 to 60 passengers.
Times: Eight-hour trips and a four-hour family trip on selected dates; call for information and reservations. Full-day trips not open to children and pregnant women.
Cost: $35 to $55 per person.
Refreshments: Bring your own.
Departs: Fisherman's Wharf, Monterey Harbor.
Miscellaneous: Debra Love Shearwater, an experienced marine naturalist who specializes in seabirds, has led natural history trips off the California coast since 1976. Her seabird and marine mammal trips are generally for serious birders, although in recent years whales have been spotted on nearly every cruise from the summer through November.

Morro Bay Tour Operators

Bob's Sportfishing

845 Embarcadero
Morro Bay, CA 93442
805/772–3340

Owner: Ralph Gunther.
Season: December 18 to March.
Boats: *Shir-Lee*, a 55-foot charter boat, 40 passengers; *Shir-Lee II*, a 65-foot charter boat, 65 passengers.

Times: Three-hour trips depart daily at 10 A.M. and 1 P.M.
Cost: $12 per person; $6 for children under 13.
Departs: Morro Bay Harbor.
Refreshments: Full galley on both boats.
Miscellaneous: Experienced captains narrate.

Central Coast Cruises

1220 Beach Street
San Luis Obispo, CA 94301
805/541–1435, 800/676–1677

Season: Mid-January to November.
Boats: M. V. *Lucille* and M. V. *Colleen*, 100-foot high-speed coastal passenger vessels, 140 passengers.
Times: Two- and three-and-a-half-hour cruises; call for times. From June to November, Monterey Bay and Channel Islands coastal cruises depart around 8 A.M. and return between 8 and 10 P.M.
Cost: Two-hour cruises—$19.95 per person, $17.95 for seniors (55 and up), $15 for children 8 to 12, children under 8 free with an adult; add $5 per person for three-and-a-half-hour Saturday cruises; full-day coastal cruises—$119.95 per person, $109.95 for seniors, $89.95 for children (return bus coach to Morro Bay and three meals included).
Departs: Morro Bay Harbor.
Refreshments: Full galley and bar.
Miscellaneous: All trips include a nature cruise along inaccessible stretches of the central coastline to view seals, sea lions, sea otters, dolphins, and marine birds.

Paradise Sportfishing

P.O. Box 356
Avila Beach, CA 93424
805/595–7200, 800/714–FISH (3474)

Owner: John Howell.
Season: Mid-December to mid-May.
Boat: *Eclipse*, a 63-foot charter boat, 49 passengers.
Times: Two trips a day on weekends and on three weekdays; call for schedule.
Cost: $15 per person; $10 for seniors (60 and up), $10 for children under 13.
Departs: Hanford Pier in Avila Beach.
Refreshments: Full galley.
Miscellaneous: Sightings guaranteed or you get a "whale check" good for another cruise. Gray whales pass right off the point,

only a few minutes outside the harbor, on their southward migration.

Virg's Sportfishing

1215 Embarcadero
Morro Bay, CA 93442
805/772–1222

Owner: Sharon Moore.
Season: December 26 to mid-March.
Boats: Five 55- to 90-foot sportfishing boats, 35 to 75 passengers.
Times: Two-hour cruises depart daily at 8:30 A.M., 11:30 A.M., and 2:30 P.M.
Cost: $15 per person; $9 for children under 13.
Departs: Morro Bay Harbor.
Refreshments: Four of the boats have full galleys.
Miscellaneous: Experienced captains and crew narrate.

Channel Islands and Santa Barbara Tour Operators

The Condor

SEA Landing Breakwater
Santa Barbara, CA 93109
805/963–3564

Owner: Fred Benko.
Season: Island whale watching (southward gray whale migration)—December 27 to February 11; coastal whale watching (northward gray whale migration)—February 12 to April 30; Channel Islands nature cruises (humpbacks and blue whales)—late May through December, depending on whale sightings.
Boat: *The Condor,* an 88-foot charter boat, 125 passengers, special "smokeless" diesels.
Times: Island whale watching—most Sundays and Thursdays from 8 A.M. to 5 P.M. (call to confirm); coastal whale watching—daily except Wednesday at 9 A.M., noon, and 3 P.M.; Channel Islands nature cruises—full-day trips (call for information).
Cost: Island whale watching—$59 per person, $30 for children under 13; coastal whale watching—$22 per person, $12 for children; Channel Islands—$65 per person, $30 for children.
Departs: SEA Landing, Santa Barbara Harbor.
Refreshments: Full galley and bar.
Miscellaneous: Captain Fred Benko, who has been in the business for more than 20 years, narrates. Outside experts narrate full-day trips.

Island Packers, Inc.

1867 Spinnaker Drive
Ventura, CA 93001
805/642–7688

Owner: The Connally family.
Season: December 26 to March 31.
Boats: *The Vanguard,* a 65-foot charter boat, 49 passengers; *The Jeffrey Arvid,* a 65-foot charter boat, 49 passengers.
Times: Half-day trips to and around Anacapa Island and full-day trips that stop on Anacapa Island. Call for schedule.
Cost: Full-day trips—$37 per person, $20 for children under 12; half-day trips—$21 per person, $14 for children.
Departs: Ventura Harbor.
Refreshments: Galley on board.
Miscellaneous: Crew members are trained naturalists. Island Packers offers daylong and overnight hiking and camping trips to the Channel Islands year-round. Humpback and blue whales are often sighted in the summer months.

SOUTH COAST TOUR OPERATORS

Oxnard Tour Operator

Cisco Sport Fishing

Captain Jack's Landing
4151 South Victoria Avenue
Oxnard, CA 93035
805/985–8511

Captain: Pete Bardini.
Season: Mid-December to April.
Boat: *Speed Twin,* 65 feet, 100 passengers.
Times: Three-hour trips depart daily at 9 A.M. and 1 P.M.
Cost: $20 per person, $15 for seniors (65 and up) and children under 12.
Departs: Channel Islands Harbor in Oxnard.
Refreshments: Full galley.
Miscellaneous: Naturalists accompany some trips; otherwise, the captain narrates.

Marina del Rey Tour Operator

The Charter Connection

14126 Marquesas Way
Marina Del Rey, CA 90292
310/827–4105

Season: December 26 to early April.
Boat: *Miss Christy*, a 47-foot sportfishing boat, 48 passengers.
Times: Three- to four-hour cruises on the weekends at 9 A.M. and 1 P.M.
Cost: $17 per person; $15 for seniors (55 and up); $12 for children 3 to 11.
Departs: Marina del Rey, Los Angeles.
Refreshments: Refreshments and snacks available.

Redondo Beach Tour Operator

Redondo Sport Fishing

233 North Harbor Drive
Redondo Beach, CA 90277
310/372–2111, 213/772–2064

Owner: Terry Turk.
Season: December 26 to early April.
Boat: *Voyager*, a 65-foot custom-built excursion boat with upper and lower viewing decks, 144 passengers.
Times: Three- to three-and-a-half-hour cruises on weekdays at 10 A.M. and 1:30 P.M. and on weekends at 9:30 A.M. and 1:30 P.M.
Cost: Weekdays—$8 per person, $6 for students; weekends—$12 per person, $8 for children under 12; two-for-one special on weekday afternoons.
Departs: Redondo Beach Marina.
Refreshments: Beverages and snacks sold on board on weekends.
Miscellaneous: American Cetacean Society volunteers narrate.

San Pedro Harbor Tour Operators

Skipper's 22nd Street Landing

141 West 22nd Street
San Pedro, CA 90731
310/832–8304

Season: January 8 to March 31.
Boats: Fleet of modern 75- to 90-foot sportfishers, 120 passengers.
Times: Two-and-a-half-hour cruises on weekdays at 10 A.M. and 1 P.M. and on weekends at 9 A.M., 11:30 A.M., and 2 P.M.
Cost: $11 per person, $8 for seniors (62 and up) and children under 13; $1 more on the weekends.
Departs: San Pedro Harbor.
Refreshments: Full galleys.
Miscellaneous: Volunteers from the Cabrillo Marine Museum narrate all trips.

Spirit Cruises and Whale Watch

Berth 75, W-33, Ports O'Call
San Pedro, CA 90731
310/548–8080

Owner: Jayme S. Wilson.
Season: December 26 to mid-April.
Boats: M. V. *Pacific Spirit*, a 65-foot motor yacht, 100 passengers; M. V. *Spirit*, a 90-foot motor yacht, 150 passengers.
Times: Two-and-a-half-hour cruises daily; several on weekends. Call for times and reservations.
Cost: $15 per person; $8 for children 2 to 12.
Departs: San Pedro and Long Beach.
Refreshments: Snacks, beverages, and cocktails are available.
Miscellaneous: Experienced captains narrate. Guaranteed sightings or you receive a free trip.

Long Beach Harbor Tour Operators

Belmont Pier

P.O. Box 14686
Long Beach, CA 90814
310/434–6781, 310/434–4434

Season: January 2 to April 16.
Boats: *The Aztec*, a 65-foot charter boat, 109 passengers; *The Enterprise*, an 85-foot charter boat, 149 passengers.
Times: Three-hour cruises daily at 10 A.M. and 1 P.M.
Cost: $8 per person ($10 on weekends), $6.50 for children under 13 ($7.50 on weekends).
Departs: Belmont Pier in Long Beach.
Refreshments: Full galleys.
Miscellaneous: Narration by experienced captains.

Catalina Cruises

320 Golden Shore
Long Beach, CA 90802
310/436–5006, 800/228–2546

Season: January to March.
Boats: Fleet of 135-foot, three-deck Catalina Island cruise boats (the largest whale-watching vessels on the coast), 500 passengers.
Times: Three-hour cruises on the weekends at 10 A.M. and 1:30 P.M.; schedule varies on weekdays, so call for times.
Cost: $14 per person; $12 for seniors (55 and up); $10 for children 3 to 11; infants under 3 free (one per adult).
Departs: Catalina Terminal in Long Beach.

Refreshments: Full bar and snack bar.
Miscellaneous: Narrators are from the Cabrillo Marine Museum.

Long Beach Sportfishing

555 Pico Avenue
Long Beach, CA 90802
310/432–8993

Owners: Veronica Wegner and Don Ashley.
Season: January 15 to April 3.
Boats: Fleet of 65- to 75-foot sportfishermen, 90 to 107 passengers.
Times: Two-and-a-half- to three-hour cruises daily at 10 A.M. and
1 P.M.
Cost: $12 per person; $9 for children under 16.
Departs: Long Beach Sportfishing, Queen's Wharf, Long Beach
Marina.
Refreshments: Onboard snack bars.
Miscellaneous: Over 15 years' experience. Knowledgeable captains narrate.

Shoreline Village Cruises

429 Shoreline Village Drive, Suite N
Long Beach, CA 90802
310/495–5884

Owner: The Wilson family.
Season: December 26 to mid-April.
Boats: *Pacific Spirit,* a 100-foot motor yacht, 150 passengers (weekdays); *Sailing Spirit,* a 90-foot sailboat, 100 passengers (weekends).
Times: Two cruises daily; call for times and departure locations.
Cost: $12 per person; $8 for children under 13.
Departs: Long Beach Harbor and the Port of San Pedro.
Refreshments: Snack bars and cocktails.
Miscellaneous: Guaranteed sightings or you get a rain check.
Spotter airplanes help the boats find whales. Experienced captains provide commentary.

Star Party Cruises

140 Marina Drive
Long Beach, CA 90803
310/431–6833

Season: January to mid-April.
Boat: *Toronado,* 75 feet, 124 passengers.
Times: Two-and-a-half-hour trips daily at 10 A.M. and 1 P.M.
Cost: $13 per person; $12 for seniors (55 and up); $10 for children
under 13.
Departs: Alameda Bay in Long Beach.

Refreshments: Full galley.

Miscellaneous: Professional narration by captain and crew.

Newport Beach/Balboa Tour Operators

Davie's Locker

400 Main Street
Newport Beach, CA 92661
714/673–1434

Owner: Doug Ferrel.

Season: December 26 to April 3.

Boat: *Western Pride,* a 77-foot charter boat, 121 passengers.

Times: Two- to two-and-a-half-hour cruises on weekdays at 10 A.M. and 1 P.M. and on weekends at 9 A.M., noon, and 2:30 P.M.

Cost: $12 per person; $10 for seniors (62 and up); $6 for children 4 to 12.

Departs: Balboa Pavilion, Newport Beach.

Refreshments: Full galley.

Miscellaneous: Narrators are from the American Cetacean Society.

Newport Landing Sportfishing

309 Palm Avenue, Suite F
Balboa, CA 92661
714/675–0550

Owners: Mike Thompson and Jim Watts.

Season: December 26 to April 10.

Boats: *Nautilus,* 72 feet and two decks, 114 passengers; *Patriot,* 76 feet, 88 passengers.

Times: Two- to two-and-a-half-hour cruises on weekdays at 10 A.M. and 1 P.M. and on weekends at 9 A.M., noon, and 2:30 P.M.

Cost: $12 per person; $6 for seniors (65 and up) and children under 13.

Departs: Newport Landing Sportfishing dock, Balboa, Newport Beach.

Refreshments: Galleys on board.

Miscellaneous: Guaranteed marine mammal sighting or you get a rain check.

Dana Point Tour Operators

Dana Wharf Sportfishing

34675 Golden Lantern
Dana Point, CA 92629
714/496–5794

Owner: Don Hansen.

Season: December 26 to mid-April.

Boats: *Seahorse*, a 65-foot charter boat, 78 passengers; a fleet of 65-foot sportfishermen.

Times: Two-hour trips on weekdays at 11 A.M., noon, and 2 P.M. and on weekends at 8 A.M., 10 A.M., noon, 2 P.M., and 4 P.M.

Cost: $12 per person; $7 for children under 13; on weekdays only, $7 for seniors (60 and up).

Departs: Dana Wharf Sportfishing Docks, Dana Point Harbor.

Refreshments: Galleys on board.

Miscellaneous: In the whale-watching business for more than 25 years. Experienced captains narrate. Guaranteed sightings of whales or dolphins or you get a free trip. It takes only five minutes to get from the wharf to the whales.

Thompson Voyages

P.O. Box 217
Laguna Beach, CA 92652
714/497–1055

Owner: Doug Thompson.

Season: January to April.

Boat: *Spike Africa*, an 80-foot two-masted sailing schooner, 30 passengers.

Times: Eight-hour cruise on Saturdays; call for dates and times.

Cost: $45 per person.

Departs: Dana Wharf Docks, Dana Point.

Refreshments: Bring a picnic lunch.

Miscellaneous: Doug Thompson is a naturalist, photographer, and writer who narrates the daylong natural history cruises on a beautiful sailing ship that's a replica of a turn-of-the-century Coast Guard cutter.

Oceanside Tour Operator

Helgren's Sportfishing

315 Harbor Drive South
Oceanside, CA 92054
619/722–2133

Owners: The Helgren family.

Season: December 26 to March.

Boats: *Electra*, 80 feet, 125 passengers; *Oceanside 95*, 98 feet, 140 passengers.

Times: Two-and-a-half-hour cruises on weekdays at 10 A.M. and 1 P.M. and on weekends at 9 A.M., 11:30 A.M., and 2 P.M.

Cost: $12 per person; $10 for seniors (60 and up) and children 12 to 15; $9 for children under 12.

Departs: Oceanside Harbor.

Refreshments: Galleys on board.

Miscellaneous: The Helgren family has been running whale-watching cruises since the early 1960s. Experienced captain narrates. If no whales or dolphins are spotted, you receive a half-fare credit on a future trip.

San Diego Tour Operators

Classic Sailing Adventures

9355 Altos Drive
Las Mesa, CA 91941
619/542–0646, 619/224–0800, 800/659–0141

Captain: Roger Anderson.

Season: Mid-December to mid-March.

Boats: *The Mariposa,* a 35-foot sailing cutter, six passengers; *The Sea Maiden,* a 35-foot sailing sloop, six passengers.

Times: Four-hour cruises daily at 8:30 A.M. and 1 P.M.

Cost: $40 per person.

Departs: Shelter Island Marina Inn, San Diego Harbor.

Refreshments: Beverages and hors d'oeuvres included.

Miscellaneous: Whale watching from a sailboat has a special charm, and the motorless approach probably appeals to the animals, too. Captain Anderson has been taking people whale watching since 1990.

H&M Landing

2803 Emerson Street
San Diego, CA 92106
619/222–1144

Owner: Phil Lobred.

Season: Mid-December to mid-March.

Boats: Several 85-foot sportfishing vessels, 100 passengers each.

Times: Three-hour cruises daily at 10 A.M. and 1:30 P.M.; five-hour cruises Thursday to Sunday at 10 A.M.

Cost: Three hours—$15 per person, $10 for seniors (55 and over) and children under 18; five hours—$25 per person, $20 for seniors and children 13 to 17, $15 for children under 13.

Departs: H&M Landing, San Diego Bay.

Refreshments: Full galley.

Miscellaneous: American Cetacean Society naturalists accompany some trips. Otherwise, experienced captains narrate. Whale sightings are guaranteed or you get a free trip. Captain Miller, one of the operation's founders, started taking friends and customers whale watching in 1935, making H&M the first whale-watching operator on the West Coast.

Islandia Sportfishing

1551 West Mission Bay Drive
San Diego, CA 92109
619/222–1164

Captain: Tim J. Voaklander.
Season: December 15 to late March.
Boat: *Dolphin,* an 85-foot charter boat, 147 passengers.
Times: Two- to three-hour cruises on weekdays at 10 A.M. and 1 P.M. and on weekends at 9 A.M., 11:30 A.M., and 2 P.M.
Cost: $12 per person; $9 for seniors (55 and up) and children under 13.
Departs: Islandia Sportfishing, Mission Bay, San Diego.
Refreshments: Full galley.
Miscellaneous: Professional naturalists narrate some cruises. Guaranteed whale sightings or you get a free trip.

Orion Charters, Inc.

3842 Liggett Drive
San Diego, CA 92106
619/574–7504

Captain: Keith Korporaal.
Season: Mid-December to mid-March.
Boat: *Orion,* a 64-foot sailing yacht built in 1934, 16 passengers; *Canadian Gal,* a 30-foot sailboat, 6 passengers.
Times: Three-hour trips on *Orion* daily at 1 P.M.; three-and-a-half- to four-hour trips on *Canadian Gal* daily at 9 A.M. and 1:30 P.M.
Cost: $39 per person; $19.50 for children under 13.
Departs: Sheraton Harbor Island East Hotel Marina, San Diego.
Refreshments: Soft drinks included. Bring your own snacks.
Miscellaneous: Captain Korporaal provides narration. He has been running sail-powered whale-watching trips since 1990.

Pacific Hornblower

1066 North Harbor Drive
San Diego, CA 92101
619/234–8687

Season: January to mid-March.
Boat: *Pacific Hornblower,* a 105-foot motor yacht, 260 passengers.
Times: Three-and-a-half-hour trips daily at 9 A.M. and 1:30 P.M.
Cost: $15 per person; $13 for seniors and military personnel; $7.50 for children under 13.
Departs: B Street Terminal, San Diego.
Refreshments: Full bar and snack bar on board.
Miscellaneous: Narration by experienced captains. Guaranteed whale sightings or you get a free trip. Over 10 years' experience.

San Diego Harbor Excursions

1050 North Harbor Drive
San Diego, CA 92101
619/234–4111

Captain: Bill Griffith.
Season: December 26 to mid-March.
Boat: M. V. *Morningstar*, 65 feet, 110 passengers.
Times: Three-hour trips daily at 10 A.M. and 1:30 P.M.
Cost: $15 per person; $13 for seniors and military personnel; $7.50 for children under 13.
Departs: San Diego.
Refreshments: Galley on board.
Miscellaneous: Guaranteed whale sightings or you get a pass good for a free weekday cruise. Captain Griffith narrates.

Seaforth Sportfishing Corporation

1717 Quivira Road
San Diego, CA 92109
619/224–7767

Owner: Frank LoPreste.
Season: Mid-December to mid-March.
Boats: *New Sea Forth*, 85 feet, 149 passengers; *San Diego*, 75 feet, 118 passengers.
Times: Two- to two-and-a-half-hour trips on weekdays at 10 A.M. and 1 P.M. and on weekends at 9 A.M., 11:30 A.M., and 2 P.M.
Cost: $12 per person; $8 for seniors (62 and up) and children under 17.
Departs: Seaforth Sportfishing dock, Mission Bay, San Diego.
Refreshments: Galleys on board.
Miscellaneous: Some trips are sponsored by the Scripps Marine Laboratory and are narrated by Scripps naturalists. Guaranteed whale sightings or your next trip is free.

RESOURCES

Año Nuevo State Reserve

Highway 1 on New Year's Creek Road
415/879–0227

Located on the coast between San Francisco and Santa Cruz, this remarkable reserve teems with thousands of giant Northern elephant seals who congregate here from December through March to breed and give birth. During this time, special guided tours bring you into the midst of these blubbery creatures. Battling, bellowing bulls compete for mates, while cows jockey for prime beach space to nurse their woolly black pups.

To make reservations during the breeding season (December to March), call Mystix Ticket Agency at 800/444–7275. Reserve at least two months in advance for a weekend tour. Entrance permits, required from April to November, can be obtained at the entrance station from 8 A.M. to 3:30 P.M. Donations are requested; $4 parking fee. Call 415/879–0852 for more information.

Harbor seals and California and Steller's sea lions also inhabit the reserve area year-round. You might see the occasional sea otter exploring the northern limits of the California sea otter range.

Cabrillo Marine Aquarium

3720 Stephen White Drive
San Pedro, CA 90731
213/548–7562

Focusing on the sea life of southern California, this aquarium has an exhibit on the gray whale migration. They sponsor whale-watching tours. Closed on Mondays, Thanksgiving, and Christmas. Admission is free, but there's a charge for parking.

California Office of State Tourism

P.O. Box 9278
Van Nuys, CA 91409
800/862–2543

Channel Islands National Park

1901 Spinnaker Drive
Ventura, CA 93001
805/658–5730

Farallones National Marine Sanctuary

Fort Mason, Building 201
San Francisco, CA 94123
415/556–3509

Friends of the Sea Lion

20162 Laguna Canyon Road
Laguna Beach, CA 92651
714/494–3050

This marine mammal veterinary facility rescues and treats stranded marine mammals and returns them to the wild. Open daily year-round; call for hours.

The Marine Mammal Center

Fort Cronkhite, Marin Headlands
Golden Gate National Recreation Area
Sausalito, CA 94965
415/289–SEAL (7325), 415/289–7330 (groups of 10 or more)

Just north of the Golden Gate Bridge, this Presidential award-winning nonprofit facility rescues sick, injured, and orphaned marine mammals and returns them to the wild. They treat hundreds of seals and sea lions on the premises each year and will travel off-site to care for cetaceans. Under the supervision of a core professional staff, volunteers carry out most of the rescuing, medicating, feeding, and treating of injuries. Patients have included California sea lions, Northern elephant seals, harbor seals, Northern fur seals, Steller's sea lions, and rare Guadalupe fur seals. One famous outpatient was Humphrey the humpback whale, whose lengthy wanderings in San Francisco Bay and up the Sacramento River drew international attention.

Visitors are welcome, and docents are available on weekends. TMMC is absolutely worth a visit if you are at all interested in marine mammals.

Marine Mammal Center

3930 Harrold Ave
Santa Barbara, CA 93110
805/687–3255

This rescue and rehabilitation center for stranded seals and sea lions covers the southern California coast. Special lectures and tours can be arranged.

Monterey Bay Aquarium

886 Cannery Row
Monterey, CA 93940
408/648–4888

One of the largest and most-visited aquariums in the world, the Monterey Bay Aquarium has superb exhibits, both permanent and temporary. A new wing, which will more than double the current exhibit space, is slated to open in 1996. Open daily year-round; call for hours. Admission fee.

Santa Barbara Museum of Natural History

2559 Puesta del Sol Road
Santa Barbara, CA 93105
805/682–4711

A blue whale skeleton is just one of the marine mammal exhibits at this museum, which sponsors whale-watching trips on the *Condor* (see listing) and offers educational programs on whales and marine life. Open daily year-round, except for major holidays; call for hours. Admission fee.

Sea Center is a branch of the museum that focuses on the marine and bird life of the Santa Barbara Channel. Located at #211 Stearns Wharf. Open daily; call 805/962–0885 for hours. Admission fee.

Steinhart Aquarium

California Academy of Sciences
Golden Gate Park
San Francisco, CA 94118
415/221–5100

Located in San Francisco's natural history museum, the Steinhart is one of the first and finest aquariums in North America. Classes on marine mammals are sometimes given. Open daily year-round; call for hours. Admission fee.

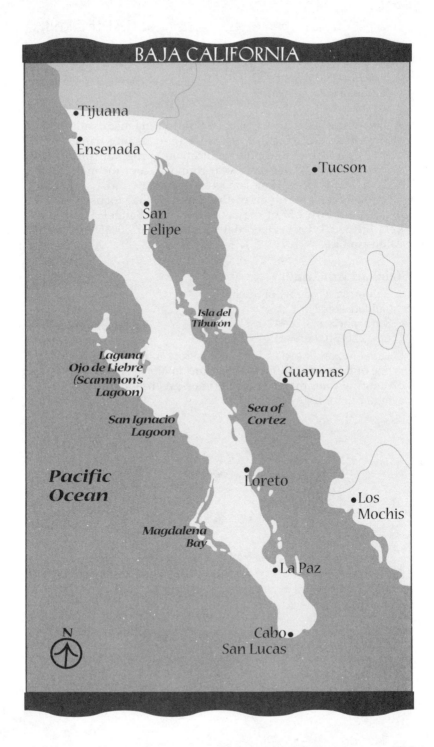

BAJA CALIFORNIA

•Tijuana

•Ensenada

•Tucson

•San
Felipe

*Isla del
Tiburón*

*Laguna
Ojo de Liebre
(Scammon's
Lagoon)*

•Guaymas

*San Ignacio
Lagoon*

*Sea of
Cortez*

*Pacific
Ocean*

•Loreto

•Los
Mochis

*Magdalena
Bay*

•La Paz

N

Cabo•
San Lucas

9

BAJA
CALIFORNIA
AND THE SEA
OF CORTEZ

Baja California and the Sea of Cortez stand in stark contrast to each other—sere desert wilderness next to deep blue seas teeming with marine life. Here you'll find what is perhaps the best whale watching in the world. The breeding and birthing lagoons of the gray whale are on Baja's west coast, where nearly 20,000 whales reside from December to April. Laguna San Ignacio and Magdalena Bay are open for controlled entry by small whale-watching boats. Laguna Ojo de Liebre, the infamous Scammon's Lagoon, where the wholesale slaughter of gray whales began in the 1850s, was declared a gray whale refuge by the Mexican government in 1972. Tour vessels approach the lagoons from the Pacific, and passengers are off-loaded into "pangas," skiffs that are operated by local fishermen and licensed by the government for whale-watching trips into the outer lagoons. The birthing areas in the inner lagoons are off-limits, but you can still see plenty of the activity from the skiffs. Boats are often approached by Baja's famous "friendlies," a small group of whales who for one reason or another find humans worthy of closer examination. Exhibiting what scientists refer to as "curious" behavior, the friendlies come right up to the skiffs, often allowing people to reach out and touch them. Sometimes they gently rub up against the boats, and have even been known to playfully lift a boat out of the water on their backs.

In the offshore Baja waters and the Sea of Cortez, which lies between Baja and the Mexican mainland, you can, in the space of a few days, see more whale species than anywhere else in the world. Blues, humpbacks, fins, minkes, Bryde's, grays, and orcas are frequently sighted, as are bottlenose and common dolphins. Less common, although still often seen, are sperm, sei, and short- and long-finned pilot whales; Risso's, spotted, spinner, and Pacific white-sided dolphins; and false killer whales. Rare species include cochito, pygmy and dwarf sperm whales, and Cuvier's beaked whales.

Baja's offshore islands, which include Todos Santos, San Martin, the San Benitos, and Cedros, are often visited by the whale-watching cruise operators listed in this chapter. These islands are inhabited by harbor seals, Northern elephant seals, California sea lions, and the Guadalupe fur seal. On Cedros and the San Benitos islands in particular, the pupping season for elephant seals coincides with the annual gray whale migration.

ONSHORE WHALE-WATCHING SITES IN BAJA CALIFORNIA

In early December the first gray whales reach the Baja coast, the end of their southward migration, which continues into February. By that time, some whales have started heading north again. The last groups to leave are the cow-calf pairs, who depart in April.

1. On the bluffs along the 80 miles of the Tijuana-Ensenada toll road are several places to view the gray whale migration. El Mirador turnoff, 20 miles north of Ensenada, offers spectacular views from 1,000 feet above the water. Punta Banda Point also has good viewing; the turnoff is located 11 miles south of Ensenada and then 13 miles northwest on the road to la Bufadora.

2. Several locations near the town of Guerrero Negro are accessible by car, including the old salt-mining wharf seven miles past town, and the Parque Natural de Ballena Gris/Gray Whale Natural Park; the turnoff is 5.6 miles south on Highway 1 from the Guerrero Negro turnoff.

3. Farther south, at Magdalena Bay, there are several onshore viewing sites. At Estero Soledad, in the northern reaches of the bay, is a viewing site on the cannery dock in Puerto Lopez Mateos. Around the town of San Carlos, there are good viewpoints near the grain elevators and at Punta Sterns, a mile hike south of town.

Baja California Tour Operators

Baja Expeditions

2625 Garnet Avenue
San Diego, CA 92109
619/581–3311, 800/843–6967; fax 619/581–6542

Owner: Tim Means.
Season: January to May.
Boats: M. V. *Don Jose,* an 80-foot long-distance charter boat, 18 passengers; *Copper Sky,* an 88-foot sailing schooner, 12 passengers.
Times: Five- to 10-day trips to gray whale lagoons and the Sea of Cortez. Tours of the lagoons involve overland transportation to onshore tent camps. On some lagoon trips, you return to La Paz via boat and cruise into the Sea of Cortez.
Cost: $995 to $1,995 per person.
Departs: La Paz and Magdalena Bay.
Refreshments: All onboard meals included.
Miscellaneous: Baja Expeditions has been running naturalist-guided trips to Baja for more than 20 years, making it one of the first operations in the region. Experienced professional naturalists accompany all trips.

Biological Journeys

1696 Ocean Drive
McKinleyville, CA 95521
707/839–0178, 800/548–7555

Director: Ron LeValley.
Season: January to March.
Boats: Several long-distance cruising boats with private cabins, 8 to 36 passengers.
Times: Four- to 12-day trips, including gray whale lagoons, offshore islands, and the Sea of Cortez.
Cost: $1,095 to $2,695 per person; ask about discounts for children.
Departs: San Diego and La Paz.
Refreshments: All meals provided.
Miscellaneous: Biological Journeys, one of the first operators in the area, has been running tours to Baja for more than 15 years. Experienced and professional naturalists accompany all trips.

Ecosummer Canada Expeditions, Ltd.
1516 Duranleau Street
Vancouver, BC, V6H 3S4 Canada
604/669–7741, 800/465–8884 (within Canada)
or
936 Peace Portal Drive
P.O. Box 8014–240
Blaine, WA 98230
604/669–7741, 800/688–8605 (within the U.S.), 800/465–8884
(within Canada)

Owner: Jim Allen.
Season: January to March.
Boats: Two-person sea kayaks, 10 guests maximum per trip; a
  motor launch transports people and kayaks to departure loca-
  tions and base camps.
Times: One- and two-week kayaking/camping trips in the Sea of
  Cortez and the Pacific gray whale lagoons.
Cost: $995 to $1,595 per person.
Departs: La Paz.
Refreshments: Meals included.
Miscellaneous: In operation since 1976, Ecosummer is one of the
  first and most experienced kayaking/camping/natural history
  tour companies, and they offer programs all over the world. A
  moderate level of physical fitness is required. Group equip-
  ment is provided.

Oceanic Society Expeditions
Fort Mason Center, Building E
San Francisco, CA 94123
415/441–1106, 800/326–7491

Season: February to April.
Boat: M. V. *Spirit of Adventure,* an 88-foot adventure cruising ves-
  sel, 32 passengers.
Times: Eight- to 12-day cruises, including Laguna San Ignacio
  and the Sea of Cortez.
Cost: $1,390 to $2,250 per person.
Departs: San Diego.
Refreshments: All meals included.
Miscellaneous: Oceanic Society Expeditions, a major nonprofit
  cetacean research and education organization, has been leading
  marine natural tours since 1972. Highly experienced naturalists
  lead all cruises.

Pacific Sea Fari Tours

2803 Emerson Street
San Diego, CA 92106
619/226–8224

Captain: Irv Grisbeck.

Season: January to April.

Boats: Two long-range sportfishing charter boats: M. V. *Spirit of Adventure,* 90 feet, and M. V. *Big Game,* 80 feet; 25 passengers each.

Times: Seven- to 12-day trips, including west coast lagoons, off-shore islands, and the Sea of Cortez.

Cost: $1,390 to $2,210 per person.

Departs: San Diego and Cabo San Lucas.

Refreshments: All onboard meals included.

Miscellaneous: Pacific Sea Fari has over 25 years' experience running natural history cruises. Professional naturalists accompany all trips. The wife of the *Spirit of Adventure*'s skipper speaks French, Dutch, German, and Spanish, as well as English, a plus for European visitors.

Sea Quest Expeditions/Zoetic Research

Zoetic Research
P.O. Box 2424
Friday Harbor, WA 98250
206/378–5767

Contact: Mark Lewis, Expedition Director.

Season: February to April.

Boats: Two-person sea kayaks, 12 people maximum per trip.

Times: Five- and seven-day kayaking/camping trips on the eastern shore of Baja, in the Sea of Cortez.

Cost: $699 to $849 per person.

Departs: Loreto.

Refreshments: All meals provided.

Miscellaneous: Zoetic Research is a nonprofit environmental research and education organization. Research biologists accompany every trip. No previous kayaking experience is necessary, but you must be physically fit.

Special Expeditions, Inc.

720 Fifth Avenue
New York, NY 10019
212/765–7740, 800/762–0003

Founder: Sven-Olof Lindblad.

Season: December to April.

Boats: M. V. *Sea Bird* and M. V. *Sea Lion*, 152-foot custom-built coastal cruise ships, 70 passengers each.

Times: Eight- to 10-day cruises in Baja California and the Sea of Cortez.

Cost: $1,900 to $4,050 per person.

Departs: Guaymas, La Paz, and Cabo San Lucas.

Refreshments: All onboard meals included.

Miscellaneous: Special Expeditions has been offering wildlife cruises worldwide since 1979, and is one of the most experienced operators in the field. All cruises are staffed by experienced professional naturalists. Zodiac inflatables take passengers closer to wildlife.

PART THREE
FIELD GUIDE
~ TO THE ~
MOST
WATCHED
SPECIES

10

WHALES, DOLPHINS, AND PORPOISES

Gray whale, California gray whale

Scientific Name: *Eschrichtius robustus*

Family: Eschrichtidae (The Gray Whale)

Hundreds of thousands of people on the West Coast witness the annual migration of the gray whale, making this the world's most watched whale. Hunted close to extinction several times since its Baja breeding grounds were first discovered by Yankee whaler Charles Scammon in the 1850s, the gray whale population has made one of the most extraordinary recoveries on record.

Identifying Characteristics

Annual migration pattern and location. Mottled appearance with patches of barnacles. Finless, low hump, and knuckled back.

Size: Males are 35 to 50 feet, 28 to 38 tons. Females are 42 to 50 feet, 34 to 38 tons. Calves are 12 to 15 feet and weigh about 1 ton.

Color: Mottled gray with numerous white, yellow, or orange patches of barnacles and parasites (whale lice) around the blow-hole, on top of the head, and on the fore part of the back. Calves are generally darker than adults and don't have barnacle patches.

Body: The scruffiest great whale. Robust body, thickest near its broad, pointed flippers. Narrow, V-shaped head with arched upper surface, straight mouth line curving down in back. From two to five deep throat grooves. No dorsal fin. Low hump about two-thirds of the way back, followed by 6 to 12 knobs or knuckles running down the tail stock. Wide, center-notched flukes.

Baleen: On each side of the upper jaw there are from 130 to 180 plates of coarse yellowish-white baleen, up to 18 inches long. Right-side plates are usually worn down due to feeding behavior.

Blow: Low, bushy, heart shaped; up to 10 feet.

Swimming/Diving: Flukes often raised high before diving. Four to six blows per minute between three- to five-minute dives. Cruises at 3 to 5 mph; maximum when fleeing 10 to 12 mph.

Feeding: The only bottom-feeding whales, they scoop and filter amphipod crustaceans from mud. Rarely feed during migration or when in winter grounds.

Social: Migrates annually to Baja lagoons for winter breeding and calving. Mother/calf pairs are the main social unit. Promiscuous mating during migration and in lagoons. Single calf is born every other year. In spring they migrate to summer feeding grounds in Alaska.

West Coast Range: The shallow coastal waters of the Bering, Chukchi, and Beaufort seas, with small populations from Oregon to southeast Alaska. Migrate to Baja California and back in the winter.

May Be Confused With: Humpback, sperm, and Northern right whales.

Status: More than 23,000 animals. Fully recovered from near extinction, they were recently removed from the Endangered Species List.

Commentary

Although the gray whale's fossil record dates back only 100,000 years, this species's unique physiological and behavioral character-istics set it apart from other whales and indicate it may be one of the oldest surviving cetacean families. Specialized behavior has made the gray whale unusually accessible and has contributed to its near extinction, as well as its extraordinary recovery.

Of all the great whales, grays are the only predominant bottom feeders. In the shallow Arctic seas of their summer feeding grounds, grays swim along the bottom, scraping the sides of their mouths in the mud, gouging out rectangular trenches and vacuum-ing up the top layer of mud and sand, which is rich in small crab-like crustaceans known as amphipods. (The common sand flea is one kind of amphipod.) Their huge tongue pumps the mud, sand, and water through the baleen, trapping the food in the sievelike fringe. This unique behavior may explain why grays are so comfortable swimming in shallow water, unlike other great whales.

Also unique to gray whales is their annual coastal migration, during which the animals stay within a few miles of shore, often coming right into the surf line. Whale watchers find this wonderfully convenient, but the behavior made grays easy targets for whale hunters operating from shore stations. The North Atlantic gray whale populations along the European and North American coasts were completely extinct by the 18th century, and in this century Japanese and Korean whalers have hunted the western Pacific populations to near extinction.

In the first half of the 19th century, whalers working at shore stations and on ships began to put considerable pressure on the gray whale population. But grays remained a difficult quarry on the open seas, and their habit of violently defending themselves and their calves from slaughter earned them the nickname "Devilfish." All that changed in 1855, when Captain Charles Scammon of the American whaling ship *Leonore* discovered their breeding grounds in Laguna Ojo de Liebre on the Pacific Coast of Mexico's Baja Peninsula. The slaughter began that year, and Ojo de Liebre was renamed "Scammon's Lagoon." Whalers soon discovered other breeding lagoons, and before long most of the population was destroyed. Once stocks were depleted, the whalers departed, and the population began to recover, only to be rediscovered and decimated again and again by waves of whalers who employed more technologically advanced methods each time. Finally, in 1946, an International Convention for the Regulation of Whaling was signed by 14 governments representing the major whaling nations and establishing the International Whaling Commission (IWC). At this time, the gray whale was put under full international protection. In 1972 the Federal Marine Mammal Protection Act granted further protection under U.S. law to gray whales, and the gray gained further protections after being declared an endangered species under the Endangered Species Act.

Since 1946 the population has undergone a miraculous recovery and is now estimated to be approaching 25,000 strong, perhaps more than they numbered when Scammon first discovered the Mexican breeding grounds. The very behaviors that almost led to their demise—following a tight migration route and returning to fixed breeding grounds—have permitted the species to rebound at the incredible rate of about 3 percent annually over the last couple

Gray Whale, California Gray Whale

of decades. Unlike other great whales whose decimated populations are scattered over vast stretches of ocean, grays stick together, giving them many opportunities for successful breeding.

The California gray whale was recently removed from the Endangered Species List, but other legislation that protects it from whaling in U.S. waters remains in effect.

The annual 12,000-mile round-trip journey of the California gray whale is one of the longest mammal migrations on earth. In early October, pregnant females leave the Bering Straits region, eager to get to the Baja lagoons by December, before their calves are born. Within weeks, mature bulls and breeding females follow. Moving at 4 to 5 mph, the whales cover about 100 miles per day, living off the thick layer of blubber they accumulated during the summer feeding season. This stored fat must sustain them (and in the case of pregnant females, their soon-to-be-born calves) until they return to the Arctic six months later.

Males and breeding females engage in courtship and mating during the entire migration. It's a boisterous, promiscuous affair, with the couples splashing about and churning up the ocean. Seafaring whale watchers are treated to such displays regularly and may be joined by dolphins, who for unknown reasons often show up when gray whales are mating.

Immature animals and juveniles of both sexes leave the Arctic last, with the latest arrivals making it to the waters and lagoons of Baja by February.

The northbound migration occurs in two distinct "pulses." The first, which lasts from mid-February to June, is led off by the newly pregnant females, who are followed or accompanied by mature bulls; they continue their courtship until they reach home. Immature cows and bulls and juveniles are the next to leave. The earliest northbound whales pass southbound stragglers without concern.

The second northward pulse begins in March and consists of mothers and their calves, who move slowly up the coast in pairs, generally hugging the shoreline, at times coming right into the surf line or just outside in the kelp beds. Along the way, mother and calf pairs will often stop and rest for a few hours or even days before continuing on, making them particularly easy to spot from onshore whale-watching locations during the late spring and early summer.

Humpback whale

Scientific Name: *Megaptera novaeangliae*

Family: Balaenopteridae (The Rorquals)

These marvelous singers and acrobats, whom Herman Melville dubbed the "most gamesome" of whales, are known for their spectacular breaching displays. Although hunted to near extinction, they are slowly making a comeback. Along with the gray whale, they are the most studied of the great whales.

Identifying Characteristics

Fleshy knobs on rostrum and lower lip. Huge flippers with white patches and serrated edges. Black-and-white coloration on flukes.

Size: Males average 47 feet; 50 feet maximum. Females average 49 feet; 53 feet maximum. Weight ranges from 25 to 45 tons. Calves are 15 feet, 2 tons.

Color: Black with white patches on flippers, ventral (bottom) surface of the tail flukes, and ventral body surfaces. Individuals are identified by their unique black-and-white patterns.

Body: Thicker than other rorquals. Biggest flippers of any whale species (up to 16 feet). Flattened head with many knobby protuberances. Small, humplike dorsal fin. From 14 to 35 broad ventral grooves, extending from the chin to the navel.

Baleen: Between 300 and 400 plates per side; from 2 to 2½ feet long; typically black.

Blow: Bushier than that of most rorquals, ending in a beautiful haze of spray; 10- to 13-foot column.

Swimming/Diving: Swimming speeds (in mph): feeding 1.2 to 2.5; cruising/migrating 3 to 9; fleeing 15 to 16.5. Blow four to eight times at 15- to 30-second intervals after long dives. Usually dive from 3 to 15 minutes, up to 25 minutes. Highly acrobatic, they may breach repeatedly, spyhop, lobtail. When diving, will arch back and raise flukes high.

Feeding: Generalists, they will eat krill and schooling fish like herring, mackerel, and cod, depending on location. Unique "bubble netting" feeding behavior. Often lunge feed at the surface.

Social: Usually found in small groups. The cow/calf pair is the basic social unit. Sometimes found in large groups of 200 or more. As part of their mating behavior, males sing the famous humpback songs on breeding grounds.

West Coast Range: Generally offshore waters of the continental United States, Alaska's Inside Passage, the Sea of Cortez, and Baja in the winter. Migrate to warmer waters in the winter, and north to their feeding grounds in the summer.

May Be Confused With: Any large rorqual and, from a distance, the sperm whale.

Status: Endangered and protected. There are less than 2,000 in the northern Pacific, but their numbers are slowly increasing.

Commentary

Despite being the slowest of the rorquals, humpbacks have enough energy to launch themselves nearly clear of the water during their spectacular breaching displays, sometimes repeating the maneuver over and over. Pairs occasionally will coordinate their leaps and breach simultaneously. Humpbacks frequently "lobtail"—lift their tail above the water and smack it down with the sound of a cannon shot. They'll also slap their huge pectoral fins on the water, or float with one or both flippers sticking up in the air.

Humpbacks can be equally athletic when feeding. In a fascinating behavior known as "bubble netting," one or more whales rise slowly underneath a group of prey fish, such as anchovies or herring. Circling slowly, they release a steady stream of bubbles, forming a cylindrical bubble curtain that traps the fish and pushes them to the surface. Practicing lunge feeding, the whales then rise from the deep toward the concentrated school of prey with their mouths open and their pleated throats distended with a huge gulp of water and scoop up the prize, sometimes lunging out of the water in the process. At times, as many as six humpbacks cooperate in herding schools of shrimp or fish and then take turns lunge feeding through the densely packed prey.

Annual migration is an important aspect of the humpback whale's life cycle. Populations of whales spend their summers in feeding grounds found mainly in northern latitudes; the largest West Coast populations inhabit Alaskan waters. Fortunately for Californians, some whales have found good feeding grounds off the

Golden State in recent years and spend their summers there. When winter sets in, the populations return to their breeding and calving grounds. The Alaskan population is actually made up of two separate groups, one that winters in the waters off Hawaii and one that winters off Baja California.

Interestingly, it appears that these two populations sing the same songs and modify them in the same way each year. The changes are apparently made on the Alaskan grounds before the singers leave, in some as yet unfathomable cooperative songwriting sessions. Because the songs are also altered on the breeding grounds, some 3,000 miles apart, the whales must compare songs when they return to Alaska in the spring. Humpback songs are probably the most complex and unique vocalizations in the animal world, consisting of precise patterns that may last from 6 to 35 minutes.

Mating takes place during the winter season, and females give birth every two or more years. A single calf is born after a 12-month gestation period, and is weaned at 10 or 11 months, at which time it is about 30 feet long.

Because humpbacks migrate along coastal paths and congregate on regular summer and winter feeding grounds around islands and in coastal waters, they were easy prey for shore-based whalers. Of the estimated 120,000 humpback whales that existed worldwide before modern commercial whaling nearly wiped them out, perhaps 10,000 remain today. Although they have been protected worldwide from commercial whaling since 1966, populations were so reduced in some regions that they have barely recovered. In the northeast Pacific, there are probably fewer than 1,000 left. Fortunately, many humpbacks are accessible to whale watchers.

Humpback Whale

Blue whale

Scientific Name: *Balaenoptera musculus*
Family: Balaenopteridae (The Rorquals)

A creature of superlatives, the blue whale is the largest animal that ever lived. It has a heart as big as a Volkswagen and a tongue the size of an elephant, and its 188-decibel call is the loudest sound made by a living being. Commercial whaling in this century almost exterminated the species, and only a few thousand remain. Recently, blue whales have been spotted regularly off the West Coast, a humbling experience that no whale watcher could ever forget.

Identifying Characteristics

Huge, to say the least. Blue-gray color. Flat, U-shaped rostrum with a ridge. Tall, tight blow. Tiny dorsal fin.

Size: From 50 to 85 feet, up to 100 feet (for the largest Antarctic females). Averaging 90 to 125 tons, sometimes surpassing 150 tons. Calves are 23 feet, 5,500 pounds.

Color: Blue-gray with light mottling, occasionally pale yellow on bottom.

Body: Huge, slim, and graceful. Flat, broad U-shaped rostrum with a single prominent ridge in front of blowholes. Absurdly small dorsal fin (1 foot), set way back.

Baleen: Each side has 400 plates of three-foot-long black baleen.

Blow: Single narrow, vertical jet; up to 30 feet.

Swimming/Diving: Swimming speeds (in mph): feeding 1.2 to 4; cruising/migrating 3 to 20; fleeing 24 to 30. Blows once every minute or two and dives for 3 to 10 minutes, 20 minutes maximum. Shows flukes just slightly when diving.

Feeding: Mainly euphausiid krill, up to nine tons per day in summer krill season. May not eat in winter, when in barren tropical waters.

Social: Generally found solitary or in pairs. Vocalizations include the loudest sound of any animal on earth, a 188-decibel

Blue Whale

low-frequency "honk," which may permit it to communicate with other blue whales over great distances.

West Coast Range: Offshore throughout range and in the Sea of Cortez. Commonly seen in recent years off the California coast near the Farallon and Channel islands.

May Be Confused With: Other large rorquals.

Status: Endangered and completely protected, with perhaps 1,500 to 2,000 in the North Pacific. Stocks are very slowly recovering from near extinction.

Commentary

Immense and graceful, blue whales were hunted mercilessly in this century. More than 300,000 were taken in the Southern Hemisphere, reducing populations there to a few thousand individuals. In the North Pacific there are perhaps 1,500 animals. Completely protected worldwide since 1965 by international agreement, blue whales are making a very slow recovery.

Blue whales migrate seasonally, moving in the summer to higher latitudes where huge swarms of zooplankton bloom in the nutrient-rich waters of the cold polar seas. In the Northern Hemisphere, blue whales eat only a few select species of these tiny crustaceans, consuming up to nine tons a day during the peak feeding months. This is a huge amount of food, but in relative terms it is estimated that blue whales consume only about four times their body weight each year, less than most terrestrial mammals, including man. The stores of fat built up during this summer feeding season serve them for the rest of the year, when they apparently eat little or nothing.

In winter months blue whales migrate toward the equator, where they breed and give birth in the warmer tropical and subtropical waters. Not much is known about their reproductive behavior (mating has never been observed), but gestation periods are probably around 11 or 12 months. Calves are about 23 feet at birth and weigh over 5,000 pounds. Each day they receive about 130 gallons of extremely rich milk from their mothers, growing incredibly fast, and are weaned at about seven months, by which time they've grown to 50 feet. Females can calve every two or three years.

Blue whales are usually seen alone or in groups of up to four animals. In recent years they have been spotted with great regularity during the summer off the Channel Islands near Santa Barbara and the Farallon Islands off San Francisco. In these cold, nutrient-rich waters, upwelling currents create plankton blooms and good feeding opportunities for blues. While it isn't certain they will keep returning, these blues have provided some spectacular whale-watching experiences to thousands of people.

Fin whale

Scientific Name: *Balaenoptera physalus*
Family: Balaenopteridae (The Rorquals)

Slim, powerful, and swift, the fin whale is almost as long as the blue whale. Whalers called them "razorbacks," for their sharply keeled tail stocks. As blue whale populations declined, whalers turned to the fin, taking almost three-quarters of a million of these magnificent creatures between 1904 and 1965. Fortunately, tens of thousands survive today.

Identifying Characteristics

Asymmetrical head coloration. Two-foot dorsal fin appears out of the water just after the blow.

Size: Males average 70 feet; 82 feet maximum. Females average 73 feet; 88 feet maximum. Both sexes weigh between 40 and 50 tons, and max out at 75 tons. Calves are 22 feet, 2 tons.

Color: Dark smoky gray with a grayish-brown back and a light underside. Highly characteristic asymmetry in head coloration: right side of lower jaw is white, left side is dark gray. Light chevron often behind head.

Body: Sleek, streamlined, powerful rorqual, almost as big as the blue. Curved fin, about two feet high, is set two-thirds of the way back near the tail. Single ridge on rostrum, narrower than that of the blue whale. Between 50 and 100 deep grooves from the throat to the navel. Small flippers. From the dorsal fin back, the body is very sharply compressed and is incredibly sleek when viewed from above. Sharp back ridge on the tail stock down to broad triangular flukes.

Baleen: Between 260 and 480 baleen plates per side, 2 feet long; front right-side baleen is white, the rest dark.

Blow: Single tall column. Very narrow at the bottom, widening at the top; 16 to 20 feet.

Swimming/Diving: The second fastest great whale. Cruises at 7 to 22 mph, 1.2 to 4 mph when feeding, and 25 to 33 mph when fleeing. Stays at surface for several minutes, taking five or six breaths, then dives for about 15 minutes, maximum 25 minutes. When surfacing, lower jaw is often seen out of the water. Rolls and hunches back when diving, almost never showing flukes.

Feeding: General feeders, they eat krill in the Southern Hemisphere; small fish, such as sardine and pollack, in Alaskan/Aleutian region; and anchovies and sometimes squid off California. Employing a unique approach to capturing prey, fin whales rush at concentrations of fish near the surface, turning on their right side at the last moment. Opening their huge mouths, they pivot around their right flipper in a grand scooping movement. The asymmetrical coloring of the fin whale's head—white on the right side, dark on the left—is directly related to this feeding technique. When on its side, the fin's head has the standard dark above/light below coloring of most surface ocean predators.

Fin whales are occasionally spotted by West Coast whale watchers throughout the region, but are most commonly seen in the Gulf of California, off the east coast of Baja, where there is a resident population.

Social: Found in groups of 3 to 7 individuals, including adult males, but 100 or more do congregate. Vocalization is a low moaning sound, 20 Hz.

West Coast Range: Offshore waters throughout range, moving farther north as summer progresses. Resident population in Gulf of California.

May Be Confused With: Blue, sei, and Bryde's whales.

Status: Endangered and protected. There are 15,000 in the North Pacific.

Commentary

The fin whale is one of the largest animals on the planet, second only to the blue. Fins are classic rorquals: sleek, streamlined, and fast. Able to exceed 25 mph in bursts, fins were much too fast to be caught by early whalers. But, like the blue whale, fin populations were decimated in this century by whalers in steam- and diesel-powered craft. However, the results weren't quite as disastrous, and the worldwide fin whale population is estimated at over 100,000, with perhaps 20,000 in the North Pacific.

The largest female fin whales are about 88 feet long and weigh 75 tons. Like most rorquals, they tend to migrate toward the poles and cold-water feeding grounds in spring, then back toward the equator in the fall. They mate in the winter when in warm waters, and after a one-year gestation a calf is born (at 22 feet and about 2 tons). Fin whales may live to be 100 years old.

Sei whale

Scientific Name: *Balaenoptera borealis*

Family: Balaenopteridae (The Rorquals)

The fastest rorqual, capable of bursts of well over 30 mph, the steel-gray sei whale was named by Norwegian whalers after the *seje* fish, or pollack, its preferred prey in Scandinavian waters.

Identifying Characteristics

Dark gray body with small, white ovoid scars. Sharp, prominent dorsal fin.

Size: Males are 40 to 50 feet; 60 feet maximum. Females are 50 to 55 feet; 65 feet maximum. Weights average 14 tons for the male and 17 tons for the female; 25 tons maximum. Calves are about 15 feet, 1 ton.

Color: Overall a dark gray, lighter on the belly. Typically small, white oval scars on body flanks and ventral surface, possibly from lamprey eels. Light and dark mottling, often described as metallic or glinting in the water.

Body: Streamlined and flat headed. Jaw is arched slightly more than in other rorquals; tip of nose turns down a bit. Between 30 and 60 throat grooves, extending only as far back as the rounded, pointy tipped flippers—fewer than other rorquals have. Small flukes relative to body size, with a median notch and pointed tips. Tall dorsal fin is set back farther than the fin whale's, not as far as the blue whale's. Single ridge on the rostrum, from the blowhole to the snout.

Baleen: About 350 baleen plates per side; metallic black, with very fine, fluffy, silky white fringes, unique to this species.

Blow: A narrow inverted cone, similar to fin and blue whales, but at 10 feet not as high.

Swimming/Diving: Fastest of all great whales, may break 30 mph when fleeing. Tend to surface horizontally, with head, back, and fin appearing at the same time, and spend more time at the surface than other rorquals. Typically two or three blows at 20-second intervals followed by a five- to six-minute dive, or five to six blows at 40-second intervals followed by a dive lasting 15 to 30 minutes. Shallow divers, they often swim just below the surface, leaving a "footprint" overhead. Dive by slightly arching their backs and slipping below the surface, rarely showing their fins.

Feeding: Feeds mainly on zooplankton but will also eat squid and small schooling fish, such as herring and anchovies.

Social: Usually small family groups of three to five individuals. Will form larger groups on feeding grounds.

West Coast Range: From central California to Alaskan seas in the summer. Winter off southern California and Mexico.

May Be Confused With: At a distance, hard to distinguish from fin, blue, and Bryde's whales of similar size.

Status: Endangered and protected.

Commentary

Sei whales weren't hunted in great numbers until the 1960s, when blue and fin whale stocks began to dwindle. Tens of thousands were slaughtered in short order. From a pre-hunting population estimated at over 60,000 in the Northern Hemisphere, fewer than 20,000 remain.

Sei Whale

Bryde's whale

Scientific Name: *Balaenoptera edeni*

Family: Balaenopteridae (The Rorquals)

Also known as the tropical whale, Bryde's (pronounced BREWdahs) is the only rorqual that avoids cold water. Its migratory pattern kept it safe from commercial exploitation until just before the whaling moratorium began.

Identifying Characteristics

Tropical/temperate habitat. Three distinctive ridges on the top of a flat rostrum, extending from tip of snout to blowholes (not always present).

Size: Males average 40 feet; 47 feet maximum. Females average 43 feet; 48 feet maximum. Both sexes average 13 tons; 22 tons maximum. Calves are 13 feet, 1 ton.

Color: Dark gray, lighter around the throat pleats, occasionally with a paler gray area on the back, in front of the dorsal fin.

Body: Typical slender rorqual body. Three ridges on top of head. Erect, pointed fin, never more than 18 inches tall. Flukes are deeply notched and pointy. Between 40 and 65 throat grooves extending far back along the abdomen to the navel.

Baleen: Between 250 and 400 short, slate gray, coarse baleen plates on each side.

Blow: Tall, thin rorqual spout; 13 feet.

Swimming/Diving: Deep divers, they often show their head when surfacing after a dive. Will approach ships out of curiosity. Arch their backs sharply before diving, like fin whales, but rarely show their flukes. Fast swimmers, with top speeds in excess of 20 mph, they frequently dart back and forth in pursuit of prey fish, just as dolphins do.

Feeding: Prefer schooling fish, such as herring, mackerel, anchovies, and sardines. Will eat krill.

Social: Not much is known about their behavior. Usually found alone or in pairs.

West Coast Range: Warm temperate waters off Mexico and the Sea of Cortez, and offshore in southern California.

May Be Confused With: Seis, minkes, and fins.

Status: Endangered and protected. Perhaps 15,000 in the North Pacific.

Commentary

The Bryde's whale is the sleekest and most streamlined of the rorquals. Often mistaken for sei whales in the past, Bryde's whales can be distinguished from other rorquals by the three distinctive ridges on top of the head.

Bryde's whales are found far offshore and in coastal waters, and there are some observable physical differences between the populations. They are the only rorqual that remains year-round in tropical and temperate waters, rather than migrating in summer to polar seas. On the West Coast they are most likely to be seen in Mexico's Sea of Cortez and off the Pacific coast of Baja. Due to their relatively small size and fast speed, Bryde's whales were not hunted extensively until the middle of this century after the stocks of larger whales were depleted. Numbers are estimated to be equal to pre-exploitation populations, estimated at 60,000 in the Northern Hemisphere. They were given full commercial protection in 1986.

Minke whale

Scientific Name: *Balaenoptera acutorostrata*

Family: Balaenopteridae (The Rorquals)

The smallest and most playful rorqual, minkes are commonly spotted in Washington's Puget Sound, where identified individuals return year after year. Total numbers have gone up, as whalers exterminated some of the species that competed with minkes for food. In 1993 Norwegian whalers resumed limited commercial hunting of minkes.

Identifying Characteristics

Small. Very pointy nose. White band on flipper is the best identifier.

Size: Males average 25 feet; 31 feet maximum. Females average 27 feet; 33 feet maximum. Both sexes average 6 to 8 tons; 10 tons maximum. Calves are 10 feet, half a ton at birth.

Color: Dark blue-gray above, lighter below. Distinctive white patch or band on flippers. Some have paler gray chevron pattern above flippers; others have two paler large patches on the flanks, behind the flippers and under the fin.

Body: Smallest rorqual. Chunky and not as streamlined as other rorquals. Narrow, very pointed rostrum with one ridge. Erect fin set two-thirds of the way back. Between 30 and 70 throat grooves running back to navel. Broad flukes relative to body length. Small, pointed flippers.

Baleen: An average of 300 baleen plates, about a foot long. Pale yellow with fine white fringes; black toward the back.

Blow: Low, indistinct, and often not visible. If visible, not much over six feet tall.

Swimming/Diving: Fast swimmers, with top speeds in excess of 20 mph, they like to approach boats and keep pace. Arch back before diving, and never show flukes. They do breach, sometimes rising clear out of the water and reentering cleanly headfirst, like a dolphin. Five to eight blows at 1-minute intervals; dives up to 20 minutes.

Feeding: In North Pacific, mainly fish, cod, and anchovies, though can filter zooplankton.

Social: Seen alone or in pairs, very curious about boats, will come up very close to investigate. Live about 50 years.

West Coast Range: Seen over entire range, often in shallow inland waters. Individuals may return to or reside in same areas over many years.

May Be Confused With: Small rorquals and larger beaked whales.

Status: Unknown, perhaps 9,000 in the North Pacific. Large Southern Hemisphere population is still hunted in limited quantities.

Commentary

Because of their small size, Minke whales were not hunted commercially until late in this century. Their numbers have actually increased substantially in the Southern Hemisphere, where the near elimination of the blue whale and the sharp reduction in other rorqual populations left minkes with little competition for krill. Protected from commercial whaling since 1986, minke whales are being hunted in small numbers for "scientific research," although it's assumed that most of the research subjects end up on tables in restaurants in Japan. Norwegian whalers, in defiance of the International Whaling Commission ban, resumed limited commercial hunting of minkes in 1993. Worldwide population is estimated at about 500,000 whales.

Right whale, Northern right whale

Scientific Name: *Eubalaena glacialis*
Family: Balaenidae (The Right Whales)

Known to the ancient Roman naturalist Pliny the Elder as the "true" whale, and to whalers as the "right" whale to hunt because of its huge oil reserves and docile nature, the Northern right whale is closer to extinction than any other great whale.

Identifying Characteristics

Callosities, light-colored, horny head patches that are crusty and infested with barnacles and whale lice. The largest of these, usually found on the front tip of the rostrum, called the "bonnet" by whalers, are unique enough to enable field researchers to identify individuals. Males have larger and more numerous callosities.

Size: Average 50 feet; maximum 60 feet. Between 60 and 70 tons, up to 105 tons. Calves are 15 to 20 feet.

Color: Black above with light callosities, often with some scars and mottling. White patches on chin and belly near navel.

Body: Robust and rotund. Huge arched head. Narrow rostrum. No throat grooves. Unlike bowheads, there's no dip behind the blowhole. Wide, paddle-shaped flippers. No dorsal fin. Broad thin flukes that are deeply notched and have pointed tips.

Baleen: Each side has 250 plates of nine-foot-long baleen, which range from light gray to black.

Blow: Two widely separated blowholes produce a wide, misty, fan-shaped spout, about 16 feet high.

Swimming/Diving: Slow swimmers, they cruise from 3 to 7 mph and when fleeing go between 7 and 11 mph. Stay on surface 5 to 10 minutes, blowing once a minute, then dive for 10 to 20 minutes. Nearly always raise and show flukes when diving. Have been seen resting motionless on the bottom for 10 minutes.

Feeding: Primarily surface feeders, right whales eat by skimming through zooplankton-rich patches of surface water with their mouths open, trapping tiny copepod crustaceans in the fine bristles of their long, narrow baleen plates. Occasionally seen bottom feeding in shallow water.

Social: Usually found in small family groups, most commonly in mother and calf pairs. Vocalizations include belches, moans, and sometimes clicks.

West Coast Range: Historically, the entire coast.

May Be Confused With: Bowhead, gray, and humpback whales.

Status: Endangered and fully protected, the right whale is very rare throughout its range. There are perhaps 200 animals left in the North Pacific, and their numbers do not seem to be recovering. They are found in small numbers in the Bering Sea, the Gulf of Alaska, and rarely, off California and the Northwest.

Commentary

Although the scientific name *Eubalaena glacialis* is derived from the Greek *eu*, meaning "true" or "right," right whales apparently earned their common name by being the "right" whales to hunt.

Their slow speed made them easy to approach and kill, and instead of sinking, their dead carcasses conveniently floated on the surface. Their huge baleen plates and thick, oil-rich blubber meant big profits.

Centuries ago, the right whale became the first of the great whales to be hunted regularly by European whalers, and they've narrowly avoided extinction ever since. Today, out of a pre-exploitation population that numbered in the scores of thousands, only a few thousand right whales remain, scattered in remnant populations around the world.

Only one right whale species, the Northern, can be seen off the West Coast, and, as there are only a few hundred of these gentle creatures in the northeast Pacific, it's a rare treat. The more common bowhead whale inhabits Alaskan waters along the edge of the polar ice cap, far to the north of our study area. The Southern right whale, which is almost identical to its northern cousin, lives in the Southern Hemisphere. The distantly related pygmy right whale is also found only in the Southern Hemisphere; only 20 feet when mature, this rarely seen cetacean is the smallest of all the baleen whales.

Right Whale, Northern Right Whale

Sperm whale

Scientific Name: *Physeter macrocephalus*

Family: Physeteridae (The Sperm Whale)

The great white whale of Moby Dick fame was a sperm whale, and its fearsome exploits were based on true accounts of these awesome, massive-headed creatures ramming and sinking whaleboats and deliberately attacking the crews. Some even sank wooden whaling ships. Loyal and protective, sperm whales form tight family groups and defend their own.

Identifying Characteristics

Huge boxlike head. Blow tilted forward and to the left. Body appears wrinkled. Low bump for a dorsal fin. Knuckled tail stock.

Size: Males are 50 to 60 feet, 45 to 70 tons. Females are 35 to 40 feet, 15 to 20 tons. Calves are 13 feet, 1 ton at birth.

Color: Dark or brownish gray. Paler gray belly and front of head. White skin around the mouth.

Body: Robust body with an enormous boxlike head that is up to one-third of body length. Blowhole at front of head. No dorsal fin, just a rounded, triangular dorsal hump two-thirds of the way back, followed by a series of bumps or knuckles down the back of the rapidly tapering tail stock. Broad, triangular, deeply notched flukes have a nearly straight trailing edge. The skin appears wrinkled or corrugated. Long, narrow underslung lower jaw has 20 to 25 large conical teeth that fit into upper jaw sockets.

Blow: Very distinctive. Low, bushy blow shoots up to 15 feet from a single blowhole at the front of the massive head, angling forward and to the left.

Sperm Whale

Swimming/Diving: Will spend extended periods on the surface swimming slowly and blowing regularly before sharply arching the back, throwing flukes high, and sounding for up to 90 minutes, although 30 to 50 minutes is typical. Usually surface near the location of the dive. Deepest diving large cetacean, they can reach depths of 10,000 feet. Capable of speeds in excess of 20 knots.

Feeding: Prefers giant deep-dwelling squid but will eat smaller squid and a variety of fish.

Social: Well-developed social structure. Basic group is a "nursery school" of females and the young, averaging 30 animals. Younger males form bachelor herds. Large bulls are usually solitary but join nursery schools in the winter to form "harems" in tropical waters. Mass strandings occur regularly.

West Coast Range: Throughout range in pelagic (deep offshore) waters.

May Be Confused With: Humpback whale, if only the flukes and back are seen. Humpback flukes are white underneath; sperm whale flukes are dark.

Status: Endangered and protected, there may be one million in the Northern Hemisphere.

Commentary

Great sperm whales are unique and fascinating creatures. Mature males are much bigger than females (a difference known as sexual dimorphism). Both sexes have a huge boxlike head. The deepest and longest diving of the great whales, they typically stay down for an hour and can dive to 10,000 feet. Their enormous head is filled for the most part with a specialized organ that contains spermaceti, a waxy solid that may act as a buoyancy regulator during those deep dives. Refined as sperm oil, it is one of the purest and finest oils on earth and one of the main reasons whalers pursued them.

Pygmy sperm whale

Scientific Name: *Kogia breviceps*

Family: Kogiidae (The Kogias)

Although the name would suggest a Moby Dick wanna-be, stranded pygmy sperm whales are often misidentified as sharks, because of their underslung jaw and gill-like crease on the side of their head.

Identifying Characteristics

Small size, sharklike head, small dorsal fin back from body midline. False "gill" on side of head.

Size: Adults, both sexes, average 10 feet, maximum to 11½ feet, 800 to 900 pounds. Calves measure about 4 feet, and weigh 120 pounds.

Color: Dark blue-gray on back and top of flippers and flukes, fading to pale gray on sides and light gray or white on belly, with pinkish cast to lighter areas.

Body: Short and thick, with small underslung mouth. Twelve to 16 pairs of sharp curved teeth in lower jaw. Head conical to square shaped. Gill-shaped marking behind mouth. Small, strongly curved dorsal fin about two-thirds back. Dolphinlike concave flukes with deep notch.

Blow: Low and inconspicuous.

Swimming/Diving: Slow-moving, deliberate. Often found motionless at the surface—tail down, head up—apparently resting. When startled, may defecate red-brown feces and abruptly dive.

Feeding: Squid, fish, crabs.

Social: Usually solitary or in small groups of 3 to 5 animals.

West Coast Range: In offshore waters from Mexico up to Washington State. Rarely observed at sea—most often seen when individuals found stranded on beaches.

May Be Confused With: Dwarf sperm whale. Very difficult to tell apart at sea—pygmy is larger, with a smaller dorsal fin set further back. Stranded animals often distinguished by tooth count.

Status: Not known.

Dwarf sperm whale

Scientific Name: *Kogia simus*

Family: Kogiidae (The Kogias)

Like the pygmy sperm whale, the dwarf sperm whale can be mistaken for a shark, although its single blowhole and lack of a true gill would be a giveaway.

Identifying Characteristics

Only recently recognized as separate species from pygmy sperm whale. Taller dorsal fin and tooth count are primary distinctions.

Size: Adults 7 to 9 feet, 300 to 600 pounds. Calves 3 feet, 100 pounds.

Color: Gray above, lightening to white below. False gill is white.

Body: Very similar to pygmy sperm whale but smaller overall. Taller dorsal fin is closer to the midpoint of the back. Dwarf sperm whales also have fewer teeth in the lower jaw: usually 8 to 11 pair vs. 12 to 16 pair in the pygmy. Dwarves may have 3 pair of small vestigial teeth in upper jaw, along with several throat grooves or creases.

Swimming/Diving: Behavior similar to pygmy. Diet indicates ability to dive to 900 feet or more.

Feeding: Squid and fish.

Social: Small groups of less than 10. Frequently found stranded.

West Coast Range: Mexico to central California, generally deeper offshore waters.

May Be Confused With: Pygmy sperm whales and some dolphin species because of dolphinlike fin.

Status: Not known.

Killer whale, orca

Scientific Name: *Orcinus orca*

Family: Delphinidae (The Oceanic Dolphins)

One of the stars of West Coast whale watching, the killer whale is really the largest dolphin. Probably the most fearsome predator on earth, the orca will eat anything that swims, and forms intelligent, coordinated hunting packs that have been known to kill great whales. However, there have been no documented attacks against humans.

Identifying Characteristics

Largest dolphin. Tall, wide dorsal fin, up to six feet high and erect in adult males. Striking white-on-black coloring, particularly white eye patch. Broad, round head.

Size: Males average 27 feet (over 30 feet maximum), up to 11 tons. Females average 23 feet (26 feet maximum), up to 8 tons. Calves are 8 feet at birth.

Color: Shiny black with white patches: small oval patch above and behind each eye; white chin and throat patch extending along belly past anus; curved flank patches behind fin. Light gray saddle patch behind dorsal fin. White undersides of flukes. Black flippers.

Body: Robust, powerful body with blunt, round head and slight beak. Large dorsal fins, falcate in females and immature males, very tall and erect in mature males (at up to six feet, the largest of all cetacean fins). Large paddle-shaped flippers.

Blow: Bushy; up to 10 feet. Often a loud, explosive sound.

Swimming/Diving: Extremely fast swimmers, exceeding 30 mph. Frequently spyhop and breach. Diving behavior varies; often a series of short dives of less than a minute followed by a longer dive lasting several minutes.

Feeding: Anything that swims or floats, except humans. Seabirds, turtles, other cetaceans (including great whales), seals and sea lions, all types of fish, and squid. Resident pods in the Pacific Northwest almost exclusively eat salmon, at least during observed months. Transient pods eat marine mammals, primarily harbor seals.

Social: Very complex and stable social structure. In Washington's Puget Sound, whales remain with their mothers in family pods of 5 to 20 animals for their entire lives. Hunt cooperatively, showing great ingenuity and intelligence.

West Coast Range: From the Sea of Cortez to Kodiak Island. Common in Puget Sound and northeast Vancouver Island.

May Be Confused With: Groups without adult males may be confused with Risso's dolphin, false killer whales, or pilot whales. Distinctive white patches should identify orcas. Dorsal fin of adult male is unmistakable.

Status: Not threatened. Reduced salmon stocks may be affecting growth of Northwest populations.

Killer Whale, Orca

False killer whale

Scientific Name: *Pseudorca crassidens*
Family: Delphinidae (The Oceanic Dolphins)
Members of this species frequently strand themselves in large numbers, often out of loyalty to a sick or injured member. Known to attack and kill other cetaceans.

Identifying Characteristics

Long, slender, nearly all-black body. Narrow, tapered head. Long, narrow "bent" flippers with curved leading edge.

Size: Males up to 18 feet, 4,000 pounds. Females to 16 feet, 2,500 pounds. Calves are 5 feet, 200 pounds.

Color: Overall, very dark gray or black, with gray blaze on chest between flippers.

Body: Long and slim; head tapers to overhanging upper jaw. Large dorsal fin in midback; usually falcate. Humplike protrusion on front of pectoral flippers.

Swimming/Diving: Fast swimmers, they often churn up the surface and leap in low arcs. Probably the largest bow riders.

Feeding: Squid and fish, including large species such as bonito and tuna. Have been observed attacking dolphins.

Social: Usually found in large groups of a hundred or more, often associating with other cetaceans. Form close group bonds.

West Coast Range: Have been spotted throughout the West Coast, although they're rarely seen north of California.

May Be Confused With: Other "blackfish," including orcas (females and juveniles) and pilot whales. Orcas have white patches and, in males, tall vertical dorsal fins.

Status: Neither abundant nor considered threatened.

Short-finned pilot whale

Scientific Name: *Globicephala macrorhynchus*
Family: Delphinidae (The Oceanic Dolphins)
These sedate "blackfish" swim slowly, loll around at the surface, rarely get excited, and never bow ride. They form strong bonds and are often the victims of mass live strandings.

Identifying Characteristics

Robust black body with bulbous head. Low, long, wide-based dorsal fin set toward head. Long, narrow, pointed flippers.

Size: Up to 20 feet, 4 tons (males larger). Calves 5 feet.

Color: Black with gray saddle patch behind dorsal fin. Pale gray anchor-shaped belly patch in front of flippers.

Body: Bulbous head, pronounced in mature males. Slight beak. Robust body, tapering behind fin to keeled tail stock. Sickle-shaped, pointed flippers. Wide-based dorsal fin sweeps back at a low angle and is set forward of body midline.

Blow: Barely visible, but the sound is explosive.

Swimming/Diving: Tend to be quiet at surface, swimming slowly. Often found resting in groups. Will spyhop. Never bow ride. Dive deeper than 2,000 feet.

Feeding: Feed at night, mainly on squid.

Social: Herds of up to several hundred are segregated into age and gender subgroups. Strong group bonds; will assist and support sick and injured individuals. Mass strandings may result. Highly vocal.

West Coast Range: Occasionally sighted as far north as Alaska, but generally prefer temperate and tropical waters from central California south. Usually found offshore, in spring they move inshore in southern California and other locations.

May Be Confused With: Other "blackfish" within range, particularly false killer whales. Short-finned pilots have distinctive bulbous head and wide, low fin set forward on body.

Status: Not threatened.

Pacific white-sided dolphin

Scientific Name: *Lagenorhynchus obliquidens*
Family: Delphinidae (The Oceanic Dolphins)

Enthusiastic bow riders and open ocean wave surfers, Pacific white-sided dolphins are found throughout the West Coast range. Although considered an offshore species, in recent years they have been seen with increasing frequency in the inland waters of the Pacific Northwest and southeast Alaska.

Identifying Characteristics

Bicolored falcate (curved, sickle-shaped) dorsal fin, thick snout, distinct black-and-white coloration.

Size: Seven to eight feet, about 300 pounds. Calves are three feet at birth.

Color: Dark gray or black back broken by white or light gray stripe along the flank, from above the eye to the anus. Also dark beak, front edge of dorsal fin, flippers, and flukes. Large gray patch above the flippers. White belly.

Body: Thick, muscular body. Tall falcate dorsal fin with dark forward edge and light trailing edge. Short beak on a porpoiselike snout.

Swimming/Diving: Fast, powerful swimmers who love to bow ride and surf. Often leap and somersault.

Feeding: Primarily squid and small fish, such as anchovies.

Social: Nearly always found in groups, usually of fewer than 50 animals but frequently in aggregations of up to 1,000 or more. Groups of 10 to 15 animals are common in inland waters.

West Coast Range: Inhabit the entire range. Although considered primarily a deepwater species, found up to 100 miles offshore, they have in recent years been seen more and more regularly close in to shore and in inland waters throughout the Northwest.

May Be Confused With: Common dolphin, Dall's porpoise.

Status: Common and not endangered. Some are harvested each year for food by the Japanese. Several thousand each year are caught in drift nets and the tuna fishery.

Commentary

Many oceanic dolphins are avid bow riders, approaching ships and hitching a ride on the bow wave, giving both whale watchers and dolphins an excellent chance to observe each other closely. Dolphins are fast swimmers and many are exuberant acrobats who leap, spin, cartwheel, and cavort in the ocean. Even scientists are forced to admit in print that this behavior may (at times, mind you) be just for fun.

These dolphins are usually found in groups, and generally the farther offshore the larger the group. Pacific white-sided and pantropical spotted dolphins form schools of several thousand animals. These species are also often found in each other's company and in the company of other cetaceans, such as pilot whales. Unfortunately, several species commonly associate with the yellowfin tuna, which is often found in large schools right below surface schools of dolphins. The purse seine tuna industry herded the dolphins into their nets to catch the tuna. In the 1970s 300,000 dolphins were dying yearly in U.S. tuna boat nets alone. Public outcry and boycotts forced the industry to adopt improved practices that trap far fewer dolphins, but foreign fishing fleets still slaughter large numbers of dolphins.

Pacific White-Sided Dolphin

Common dolphin

Scientific Name: *Delphinus delphis* and *Delphinus capensis*

Family: Delphinidae (The Oceanic Dolphins)

This beautiful animal was the dolphin of ancient Greek art and legend, first classified and described by Aristotle. Boisterous acrobats found in huge herds on the open sea, they do not take to captivity.

Identifying Characteristics

Size: Seven to eight feet, up to 300 pounds (males are slightly larger than females). Calves are three feet at birth.

Color: North Pacific population displays a black back beginning at the beak and extending to the middle of the tail stock. Just below the dorsal fin, the black area forms a distinctive V-shaped saddle, which combines with the gray, tan, or ochre flank coloring to form this species' characteristic hourglass pattern on the side. The top of the prominent beak is also black, and they have black "spectacles" around the eyes. Pale gray tail stock. Black dorsal fin may have a pale gray center.

Body: Sleek, streamlined body with tall, pointed dorsal fin. Long, clearly defined beak. Tapered, pointed flippers and concave, notched flukes.

Swimming/Diving: Swift, playful swimmers who enjoy bow riding and leaping. Usually stay near the surface but may dive to nearly 1,000 feet in search of food.

Feeding: Fish and squid. Tend to feed toward the evening.

Social: Highly gregarious, they are usually found in large boisterous schools of several hundred to several thousand individuals.

West Coast Range: Found mainly in offshore waters below the Oregon-California border, becoming more common farther south.

May Be Confused With: Striped dolphin. Look for the common dolphin's distinctive dark saddle.

Status: Not endangered. Large numbers have been killed by tuna fishers in the eastern North Pacific. Better controls are in place now.

Bottlenose dolphin

Scientific Name: *Tursiops truncatus*

Family: Delphinidae (The Oceanic Dolphins)

Stars of TV, film, and the marine show stage, bottlenose dolphins are powerful, muscular animals found in all the world's oceans. They have extraordinary echolocation abilities, which some researchers theorize are used to "see" into each other's bodies to read mood and health. Size, body shape, and coloration vary between regions and between offshore and coastal populations.

Identifying Characteristics

Looks like TV's "Flipper." Overall grayish-brown back and sides. Distinct crease at base of beak. Coastal locations. Friendly and curious behavior around humans.

Size: Six to 12 feet, up to 1,400 pounds (males are larger than females). Calves are 3 to 4 feet at birth.

Color: Dark gray to brownish-gray cape on top, shading to lighter gray sides and a lighter belly. Pink area around anus. Dark facial and eye/flipper stripes. Dark pectoral flippers.

Body: Large and usually robust dolphin. A chunky body and a medium-short snout with a crease at the base. Tall, falcate dorsal fin in center of back.

Swimming/Diving: Strong swimmers, who reach about 25 mph at top speed. Bow riders, wave surfers, and acrobatic jumpers. Usually feed in waters shallower than 300 feet but may dive to 2,000 feet.

Feeding: Very general feeders, they'll eat small fish, shrimp, squid, rays, eels, and mullet. They hunt cooperatively, herding fish.

Social: Fluid groups of 2 to 20 animals inshore, up to 1,000 offshore. Females help each other with birthing and child care.

West Coast Range: Most common in southern part of range, up through central California. Prefer temperate waters.

May Be Confused With: Other dolphins. Bottlenose dolphin lacks striping/contrasting coloration of other species.

Status: Although not threatened, they are hunted in some parts of the world and get caught in fishing nets in their West Coast range.

Pantropical spotted dolphin

Scientific Name: *Stenella attenuata*
Family: Delphinidae (The Oceanic Dolphins)

These small, fast dolphins make the fatal mistake of associating with yellowfin tuna, and during the 1970s they died by the hundreds of thousands in tuna nets. Think of them when you reach for your next can of dolphin-free tuna.

Identifying Characteristics

Spotted slender body. Narrow, pointed, falcate dorsal fin. Associate with schools of tuna.

Coloring, size, shape, and behavior vary between coastal and offshore populations.

Size: Up to eight feet, 250 to 300 pounds (males are larger than females; coastal populations are larger than offshore). Calves are about three feet at birth.

Color: Dark slate gray cape and fin, lighter gray sides and belly. Many white spots (spotting is greater with age and in coastal populations). White lips and tip of beak. Dark band from flipper to lower jaw.

Body: Slim and streamlined (coastal populations are more robust). Dorsal fin is narrow, tall, falcate, and pointed. Crease at base of beak.

Swimming/Diving: Fast swimmers (25 mph) and bow riders. High leapers.

Feeding: Anchovies, herring, other small fish, and squid.

Social: Offshore schools have several hundred to a thousand animals. Coastal schools are smaller.

West Coast Range: Sea of Cortez and Baja.

May Be Confused With: Other beaked dolphins. In West Coast range, mature animals can usually be distinguished by spotting.

Status: Probably a couple million in the Pacific. Still hunted for human consumption in Japan and the Solomon Islands.

Striped dolphin

Scientific Name: *Stenella coeruleoalba*

Family: Delphinidae (The Oceanic Dolphins)

Striped dolphins are usually found in large schools of several hundred animals. Hunted off the coast of Japan for food, they are also one of the species that gets caught in tuna nets.

Identifying Characteristics

Contrasting light blaze and dark point under tall, curved dorsal fin. Thin dark stripe from beak around eye to anus, separating gray sides from white belly.

Size: Eight to nine feet, up to 340 pounds (males are slightly larger). Calves are three feet at birth.

Color: Gray back of varying hues; white belly. Two thin black stripes lead back from the eye, one fading out over the flipper, the other running back to anus (thicker stripe from eye to flipper). Light gray chevron on flank under fin.

Body: Typical of stenella and delphinus species: slim and torpedo-shaped with a tall, falcate dorsal fin, and a moderate beak with a distinct crease at melon.

Swimming/Diving: Fast swimmers, they sometimes bow ride. They make long, clean leaps; at times, mothers and calves leap in unison. Easily spooked—a whole herd may abruptly alter course and flee.

Feeding: Small mid-ocean fish, also shrimp and squid.

Social: Found in large herds of several hundred to several thousand animals. Herds are often segregated by age and sex: females and calves, immature animals, and mature males.

West Coast Range: Mainly offshore, more common in southern part of range, uncommon north of California border.

May Be Confused With: Other dolphins. Common dolphin is the most similar, but has unique hourglass markings.

Status: Not threatened; there are perhaps a million in the North Pacific. Some are caught by tuna fishers. Thousands are taken each year in Japan for food.

Spinner dolphin

Scientific Name: *Stenella longirostris*

Family: Delphinidae (The Oceanic Dolphins)

The whirling dervish of dolphins, this aquatic acrobat leaps high and spins like a top on its long axis. Dental note: Spinners have more teeth than any other cetacean, more than 200 on average.

Identifying Characteristics

Long thin beak. Dark eye-to-flipper stripe. Unique high spinning leaps and other aerial displays. Triangular or forward-canting dorsal fin. Four subtypes recognized for the eastern tropical Pacific, with differences in form and coloration.

Size: Up to seven feet, 200 pounds (males larger). Calves 2½ feet.

Color: Main form has a dark gray back, light gray sides, a white belly, and a dark gray band from the eye to the dark gray flipper. Costa Rican form is a uniform gray with white genital patches.

Body: Slim, with long thin beak, gently sloping rostrum with definite crease. Erect, falcate dorsal fin can cant forward in older males and Costa Rican form. A thick keel may develop in the tail stock of older males.

Swimming/Diving: One of the most acrobatic and playful dolphins, it spins on a longitudinal axis while leaping high in the air. Enthusiastic bow riders.

Feeding: Small fish and squid.

Social: Herds of a few dozen up to several thousand animals. Commonly found following tuna.

West Coast Range: Offshore near southern Baja California.

May Be Confused With: Depending on color of spinner dolphin, may resemble other dolphins within the range. Very long, narrow beak, forward canting dorsal fin, and unique barrel-roll leaps should distinguish spinners from other dolphins.

Status: Many thousands were killed annually by the tuna-fishing industry until practices were changed. Some are still killed each year. Population is probably several hundred thousand.

Northern right whale dolphin

Scientific Name: *Lissodelphis borealis*

Family: Delphinidae (The Oceanic Dolphins)

Fast and graceful, these uniquely finless dolphins put on beautiful displays of synchronized fleeing when startled by an approaching boat, bunching together and speeding off with long, low, arching leaps.

Identifying Characteristics

Long, slim body, no dorsal fin. Black with white belly.

Size: Females grow to 7½ feet; males grow to 10 feet. Average 150 pounds; 250 pounds maximum.

Color: Black with white bellyband from throat to flukes, widest between the black flippers and continuing to bottom surface of flukes. Small white patch just behind tip of bottom jaw.

Body: Only dolphin without a dorsal fin off the West Coast. Slimmest of all dolphins, with long tapering tail stock. Short beak.

Swimming/Diving: Fast swimmers who can exceed 25 mph. May bow ride, but usually flee boats, bunched together and making long, low graceful leaps.

Feeding: Mainly squid and lantern fish off southern California. In other locations, a variety of fish and squid.

Social: Groups average 100 to 200 animals, up to several thousand. Often found with other dolphins.

West Coast Range: From Baja to British Columbia, usually offshore but may come in close at times.

May Be Confused With: Easily distinguished from other small cetaceans. They can be confused with leaping sea lions from a distance.

Status: Abundant within their range. They are hunted in Japanese shore fisheries. In the North Pacific, drift nets trapped thousands each year until recently.

Risso's dolphin

Scientific Name: *Grampus griseus*

Family: Delphinidae (The Oceanic Dolphins)

Also known as the grampus, these blunt-headed dolphins seem to be smiling at some private joke. The extensive scarring on their backs probably comes from mating fights with their own kind.

Identifying Characteristics

Heavily scarred gray or white body. Blunt, beakless head. Large dark dorsal fin.

Size: Average 10 to 13 feet, 600 to 700 pounds (1,000 pounds maximum). Calves are 5 feet at birth.

Color: Dark to light gray back and sides, lightening with age to almost white on head. Many white scars and scratches, mostly forward of dorsal fin. White belly patch; white anchor-shaped chest patch. Dark flippers, flukes, and (usually) dorsal fin.

Body: Stout cylindrical body tapering behind dorsal fin to narrow tail stock. Blunt, beakless rounded head with small melon and distinctive vertical crease on forehead. Tall falcate dorsal fin in middle of back; long pointed flippers.

Swimming/Diving: Sometimes quietly roll at surface, at other times very active: leaping, tail and flipper slapping, spyhopping, etc. Occasionally bow ride.

Feeding: Squid and octopus; some fish.

Social: Sometimes solitary or in pairs, usually herds of 25 to several hundred. Often associate with other cetaceans, particularly pilot whales.

West Coast Range: Through entire range to Gulf of Alaska, usually offshore in waters deeper than 300 feet.

May Be Confused With: Other dolphins or small whales, at a distance. Light color and rounded head should distinguish them.

Status: Not threatened or hunted much in West Coast range; occasionally caught in fishing gear.

Harbor porpoise

Scientific Name: *Phocoena phocoena*
Family: Phocoenidae (The Porpoises)

The Romans called this chubby little cetacean *porcus piscus,* which means pigfish. A popular menu item in medieval Europe, they were often the main dish at banquets given by Henry VIII of England (who ended up resembling them).

Identifying Characteristics

Smallest cetacean in its range. Beakless, chunky body. Inhabits shallow waters. Quiet and shy.

Size: Average 5 to 6 feet, 100 to 150 pounds. Calves are 2½ feet, 12 pounds.

Color: Dark gray to black on back with lighter gray sides and white belly. Gray stripe from corner of mouth to dark flippers.

Body: Small, rotund body. Short flippers with rounded tips. Low triangular dorsal fin with wide base.

Swimming/Diving: Shy, they tend to stay away from boats. Rarely seen jumping clear of water, though may splash considerably when moving fast in a group.

Feeding: Wide variety of small fish and squid, usually herring, mackerel, sardines, and pollack.

Social: Commonly live in small groups of 2 to 10, occasionally in larger aggregations.

West Coast Range: From southern California to Gulf of Alaska. Prefers cold water. Stays near the shore, in bays, harbors, river mouths, and estuaries.

May Be Confused With: Other dolphins, though its short fin, shallow-water locations, and shy behavior should make the harbor porpoise easy to spot.

Status: Abundant. Some mortality from fishing equipment. May be sensitive to local pollution in coastal habitat.

Dall's porpoise

Scientific Name: *Phocoenoides dalli*
Family: Phocoenidae (The Porpoises)

Stubby, muscle-bound marine hot rods with cool black-and-white paint jobs, Dall's porpoises run down boats to bow ride.

Identifying Characteristics

Stocky black body with large white section on flanks and belly. Small triangular dorsal fin with white patch. Fast swimmer, throwing up "rooster tail" of spray; bow riding behavior.

Size: Six to eight feet, up to 400 pounds. Calves three feet.

Color: Black with prominent white patch on sides and belly. Most dorsal fins black and white, some entirely black or white. Trailing edge of flukes often white.

Body: Very thick and robust; powerfully built. Small pointed flippers; small triangular dorsal fin; broad flukes. Small beakless head. Some have pronounced keel on tail stock.

Swimming/Diving: Perhaps the fastest small cetacean (35 mph), they kick up a heavy rooster tail of spray as they briefly surface. Enthusiastic bow riders. Believed to dive deeply.

Feeding: Wide range of fish: saury, hake, herring, mackerel, lantern fish. Also squid and crustaceans.

Social: Usually groups of 10 to 20 inshore, but aggregations up to several thousand are spotted in the open ocean.

West Coast Range: Common offshore and inshore through most of the range from southern California through Alaska.

May Be Confused With: When rolling slowly at the surface, may look like harbor porpoises. Reported as "baby killer whales."

Status: Not threatened in range. Were being killed by the thousands in largely discontinued drift net fishery in northern Pacific.

Cuvier's beaked whale

Scientific Name: *Ziphias cavirostris*

Family: Ziphiidae (The Beaked Whales)

Ranges from the tropics to temperate and near-polar waters.

Identifying Characteristics

Robust body. Small head with short, ill-defined beak.

Size: Males to 24 feet, females slightly smaller. Maximum weight is about 6,600 pounds. Calves 8½ feet.

Color: Calves and juveniles are tan to rusty brown; adult males have lighter heads to nearly white. Lighter undersides. White linear and oval scars.

Body: Gently curved mouth line; short beak; steeply sloping bulging forehead (melon). Paired throat grooves. Dorsal fin is relatively tall (to one foot) and varies from triangular to somewhat curved; it is set well behind midback. The pectoral fins are small.

Blow: Low and indistinct. Projects slightly forward and left.

Swimming/Diving: Vigorous swimmers who dive for over 30 minutes; raise flukes high going into dive.

Feeding: Primarily squid, deepwater fish, and crustaceans.

Social: Often found in groups of 3 to 10 animals, usually including at least one adult male, but sometimes are seen alone. Calving season is not known.

West Coast Range: Southern Bering Sea to equator. Of all beaked whales, Cuvier's may have the most extensive range, from deep tropical oceanic waters up to polar seas.

May Be Confused With: Other beaked whales, minke whales.

Commentary

Because of its wide range and more frequent strandings than other beaked whales species, scientists may learn a great deal about beaked whales in general by examining beachcast Cuvier's beaked whales. However, population numbers and potential impacts are still insufficiently known about this species.

Baird's beaked whale

Scientific Name: *Berardius bairdii*

Family: Ziphiidae (The Beaked Whales)

Baird's beaked whales are big—over 40 feet and 12 tons—but somehow never made the "Great Whale" team.

Identifying Characteristics

Largest of beaked whale family; relatively slender.

Size: Males average 34 feet, 10 tons. Females average 37 feet, 12½ tons. Calves average 14½ feet at birth.

Color: Grayish-brown; light scarring is common. Underside may have light colored blotches.

Body: Cylindrical and relatively slender. Long, well defined rostrum. Dorsal fin is small and triangular, and set well back (two-thirds of the way) on the body. Pectoral fins are small and rounded. Two V-shaped grooves on the throat. Center notch on fluke is either slight or missing altogether.

Blow: Low, round, relatively visible for a beaked whale.

Swimming/Diving: Take three or four breaths at surface at 20-second intervals before diving for 20 minutes or more. Flukes may be raised when diving; beak may be evident when resurfacing. Pods may surface and dive together.

Feeding: Deepwater species such as squid and other cephalopods, bottom-dwelling fish, and crustaceans.

Social: Gregarious, usually found in well-organized pods of 5 to 20 animals, but larger groups have been recorded, up to about 50. Can be seen sliding over one another when at surface.

West Coast Range: Found only in the North Pacific, and the Bering and Okhotsk seas in deep water (over 3,000 feet). Prefer seamounts, the continental slope, and submarine canyons.

May Be Confused With: Other beaked whales, minke whales.

Commentary

As with other beaked whales, Baird's beaked whales are little studied, being found far offshore in deep water. Their total population is unknown, and stocks in areas where beaked whale fisheries were conducted, mostly off Japan, may be depleted.

Hubbs' beaked whale

Scientific Name: *Mesoplodon carlhubbsi*

Family: Ziphiidae (The Beaked Whales)

The numerous white scars on male Hubbs' beaked whales may bear witness to encounters with other males' formidable tusks.

Identifying Characteristics

In adult males, conspicuous white beak, white raised "cap" forward of blowhole, and large flattened tusk emerging above upper beak line.

Size: Adults 17 to 18 feet and 3,300 pounds; newborn calves are about 8 feet long.

Color: Males uniformly dark gray to black with lighter scratches; heavy scarring among adult males. Females have lighter sides and bellies, less extensive scarring. Oval white scars may be seen.

Body: Robust, streamlined body. Beak is prominent and lighter colored, tapering gradually to head. Two throat grooves. Dorsal fin is curved and set two-thirds back; pectoral fins are small and tapered. Flukes have no distinct median notch.

Teeth: In adult males, two tusks erupt from gumline, set midway back on highly curved jawline, protruding above upper line of beak.

Blow: Small, rounded, inconspicuous.

Swimming/Diving: Little observed, but like other beaked whales, are presumed capable of deep, extended dives. Shy around vessels.

Feeding: Deepwater species, primarily squid and pelagic fish.

Social: Not very gregarious, traveling in groups of 2 to 10.

West Coast Range: Believed limited to North Pacific, from southern California to central British Columbia, in deep water along continental slope and seamounts.

May Be Confused With: Other beaked whales, minke whales.

Status: Not much is known about living Hubbs' beaked whales.

Blainville's beaked whale

Scientific Name: *Mesoplodon densirostris*
Family: Ziphiidae (The Beaked Whales)

This wide-ranging mesoplodont has stranded from Nova Scotia in the north to Tasmania in the south, but mostly in temperate and tropical climes.

Identifying Characteristics

Size: Both sexes can reach 15½ feet, weigh 2,200 pounds. Newborn calves just over 8 feet.

Color: Adults gray-blue above, pectoral fins lighter, underparts whitish; flukes dark on top, lighter below. White linear scars and small oval scars seen on both sexes; more extensive scratching and sometimes reddish pigment seen on heads of adult males.

Body: Spindle-shaped body, highly arched lower jaw. Prominent beak slopes gradually to flattened forehead; depression in front of blowhole. Paired throat grooves. Dorsal fin ranges from triangular to slightly curved and is situated just behind the back's midpoint. Pectoral fins small, originating in lighter pigment area of sides.

Blow: Small, indistinct, and inconspicuous.

Swimming/Diving: Have been seen swimming slowly and can dive for over 20 minutes. Upon surfacing, the rostrum may slap awkwardly on surface.

Feeding: Feed on squid primarily, may take other deepwater fish.

Social: Not very gregarious; found in small groups of 3 to 7 but also singly and in pairs.

West Coast Range: This may be the most widely distributed beaked whale, found in temperate and tropical oceanic waters all over the world, mainly in offshore deepwater habitats.

May Be Confused With: Other beaked whales, minke whales.

Status: Not enough is known about this species' status.

Stejneger's beaked whale

Scientific Name: *Mesoplodon stejnegeri*

Family: Ziphiidae (The Beaked Whales)

So elusive are these beaked whales that few have been seen alive, but frequent strandings in the subarctic to cold temperate North Pacific have yielded much of what is known about this species.

Identifying Characteristics

Dark, cylindrical body with light scarring; triangular dorsal fin set well back.

Size: Average adult reaches 16 feet, 1.3 tons (male and female).

Color: Dark gray to black with light scarring, especially in males. Underside light gray to whitish. Oval-shaped and linear white scars common.

Body: Very streamlined, with beak tapering to flat forehead. As with other beaked whales, has paired throat grooves. Dorsal fin is slightly curved, and set two-thirds of the way back on body. Pectoral fins small and dark, contrasting with lighter undersides.

Teeth: Teeth erupt from gumline only in males; a singe flattened tusk set midway back on both sides of arched lower jaw, pointing forward and extending above rostrum.

Blow: Round, low, inconspicuous.

Swimming/Diving: Shallow dives may precede longer dives of 10 to 15 minutes.

Feeding: Known to eat squid, may take other bottom-dwelling fish.

Social: Can be found in groups of 5 to 15 animals of varying ages, and may dive and surface together.

West Coast Range: Southern California to Bering Sea, west to Sea of Japan. This species frequents deepwater habitats above continental slope, seamounts, and submarine canyons near shore.

May Be Confused With: Other beaked whales, minke whales.

Status: Insufficient information is available on population size.

11

SEALS,
SEA LIONS,
AND
SEA OTTERS

Harbor seal, common seal

Scientific Name: *Phoca vitulina*

Family: Phocidae (The True Seals)

Harbor seals are the most commonly encountered of the phocid, or "true," seals, remaining close to their home turf year-round.

Identifying Characteristics

Round, torpedo-shaped body. Frequently hang vertically at the surface, a behavior known as "bottling." Often seen resting on side with head and hind flippers raised and body in crescent-shaped profile.

Size: Adults of both sexes are about six feet long and weigh about 250 pounds; pups weigh 18 to 19 pounds at birth.

Color: Ranging from almost white with dark spots, to mottled gray, to very dark gray with white spots.

Body: Plump, sleek body. Round catlike head with no external ears. Fore flippers have nails at the end. Short hair.

Behavior: Harbor seals haul out in groups ranging from a few up to several thousands. Generally solitary at sea, but young pups often hitch piggyback rides from mom. Shy and easily disturbed on land, but may approach swimmers. They are able to dive to depths of 600 feet and typically remain submerged for 5 to 8 minutes, but can stay down as long as 25 minutes. Tend to submerge "feet" first. Swim with full-body sculling motion. Not usually vocal, but adults emit snarls at encroachers. Very young pups make a wistful "ma" sound.

Preferred habitats are low, flat beaches; flat offshore rocks; and sandbars. Remain near the coast and may travel up estuaries and rivers.

Feeding: A wide variety of fish, crustaceans, and squid.

Social: Gregarious, but always keep some distance from each other at haul-outs. Will often raise a flipper to warn others away if approached too closely. Sexually mature at about three to five years. Breed in spring in southern portion of range and in summer in northern range. Pups weaned at four to six weeks.

West Coast Range: Baja California to Alaska.

May Be Confused With: Young elephant seal, spotted seal.

Status: Flourishing everywhere but in Alaska. Some native Alaskans still hunt harbor seals, and net entanglement is a problem in fishing grounds. Chemical pollution could pose a significant health threat to harbor seals, because of their coastal habits and the fact that they accumulate toxins in their blubber; a resultant weakened immune system could lead to greater susceptibility to disease.

Commentary

Harbor seals and elephant seals are phocid, or true, seals, well adapted to an aquatic environment. Their streamlined bodies lack external earflaps and their fore flippers are short and broad with nails on the end of each digit. Seal bodies are round and plump, and they cannot rotate their hind flippers forward for walking. They move gracefully through water, propelled by a full-body sculling action, using the fore flippers for steering. Their movement on land is a clumsy series of lurches, a "caterpillaring" gait. True seals typically nurse their young for a short period, weaning them at about three to six weeks. As with most phocid species, there is generally little visible difference between mature male and female harbor seals.

Northern elephant seal, sea elephant

Scientific Name: *Mirounga angustirostrus*

Family: Phocidae (The True Seals)

The biggest, deepest diving, and altogether gnarliest of pinnipeds, elephant seals spend more time underwater than some whales. Coming back from near extinction, these blubbery behemoths can be observed at Año Nuevo State Reserve south of San Francisco. They're popular; make reservations well in advance.

Identifying Characteristics

Huge body. Large proboscis (nose) on adult male. Highly migratory.

Size: Male is about 15 feet, 2 tons. Females average 10 feet, 1,800 pounds. Newborn weigh between 65 and 70 pounds.

Color: Black at birth, silvery when weaned, and gray to light brown as adults. The only eastern Pacific pinniped to molt not only their hair but their skin, after which their color appears patchy.

Body: Torpedo-shaped body covered with short hairs. Adult male has elephantlike trunk, or proboscis; females and young have short, rounded muzzle. Lack external ears. Short fore flippers have nails at edge; hind flipper nails are set back.

Behavior: Spend most of their lives at sea and are seen by humans almost exclusively at rookeries. Haul out only twice a year, to breed and to molt. Young seals engage in mock battles and are highly vocal. Can be seen flipping sand over their backs to cool their skin. When hauled out, elephant seals will often lie directly against or on top of one another. Threat vocalization of adult males is hollow, drumlike rattle. Adult females have deeper gurgling vocalization. Pups squawk like huge chickens. Elephant seals have poor mobility on land and use low, flat beaches as haul-outs.

Like most phocid seals, they swim with a sculling motion, propelling themselves with hind flippers and steering with fore flippers. They can dive to depths from 1,500 to 5,000 feet; they typically remain submerged for 20 minutes, but hour-long dives have been recorded in this species.

Feeding: Deepwater fish, such as ratfish and dogfish, and whiting, squid, and octopus.

Social: Solitary at sea, they haul out in great numbers for the breeding season and at specific seasons to molt. In breeding rookery an "alpha," or chief bull, will be surrounded by up to 50 females and their pups; he will drive away potential contenders. Males often have spectacular and bloody battles at breeding time, on the rookery and in nearby waters.

West Coast Range: Baja California to Alaska.

May Be Confused With: Pups resemble harbor seals; adults resemble the Pacific walrus.

Status: There are now more than 120,000 Northern elephant seals in the eastern North Pacific. The population is increasing throughout its range, and is extending its range northward. This rebound (from about 100 animals at the turn of the century) is a result of federal protection. Some net entanglement occurs.

Commentary

At Año Nuevo State Reserve in California, rookery tours provide a unique opportunity to observe and learn about the breeding habits of this and other species of seal.

California sea lion

Scientific Name: *Zalophus californianus*

Family: Otariidae (The Eared Seals)

Playful, noisy, acrobatic, exuberant, highly adaptable, and quick to learn, California sea lions are the "trained seals" of circus fame. Their best performances, however, are their improvised antics in the wild.

Identifying Characteristics

Medium to large, sleek body with distinct neck and doglike head. Often active and playful at haul-outs.

Size: Males typically reach eight feet in length and weigh about 800 pounds. The average female is five feet long and 250 pounds. Newborns average 2.6 feet and 13 pounds.

Color: Ranging from tan to chocolate; may appear black when wet.

Body: Head has pointed muzzle, and their profile and expression are described as "doglike." Long, flexible whiskers (vibrissae) and external ears (pinnae). Short hair; long leathery, scallop-edged flippers with nails set back from edge. Adult males develop sagittal crest, or bump, on top of head, sometimes lighter in color.

Behavior: When resting, they often sit on rocks or beaches, nose pointed skyward, or may lie on top of one another (and on elephant seals, too). Playful. Sometimes seen thoughtfully scratching neck with hind flipper. At sea, may "raft," or lie in groups at the surface with flippers extended above water, to regulate body temperature. May "porpoise"—leap clear of the surface in repeated arcs either alone or in a "chorus line." When swimming, their long fore flippers make powerful strokes, and they can reach up to 25 mph. Can dive to 450 feet and remain submerged 20 minutes.

Very vocal; they repeatedly bark like dogs, especially at haul-outs. Pups have bleatlike vocalizations. Sea lions are nimble on land and use a variety of habitats; they can climb to dizzying heights on rocky haul-outs.

Feeding: California sea lions are opportunistic feeders, preying on schooling fish, rockfish, squid, flatfish, hake, lamprey, dogfish, and salmon. They are fast pursuit-feeders.

Social: Gregarious both on land and in the water. Haul out in huge numbers in seal rookeries. Very playful, but males will chase or stare down rivals, and younger animals will practice sparring skills.

West Coast Range: Baja California to Alaska.

May Be Confused With: Steller's sea lion.

Status: Despite hunting during the 1800s and ongoing conflicts with commercial and sports fisheries, this healthy population is increasing throughout its range. In California, Oregon, and Washington there are approximately 67,000 sea lions.

Commentary

Captive California sea lions act as "ambassadors" for marine mammals in general, because they are so widely displayed in zoos and oceanaria. Observing them in the wild, however, offers far greater insights into how they relate among themselves, rather than playing to a human audience.

Sea lions and fur seals are otariids, have external earflaps, and can rotate their hind flippers under their body to move quickly on land. They are master swimmers and underwater acrobats, using their long fore flippers to speed through the water. Their muzzle is somewhat doglike. Otariid mothers typically nurse their young for six months to over a year.

Steller's sea lion, Northern sea lion

Scientific Name: *Eumetopias jubatus*

Family: Otariidae (The Eared Seals)

Distinguished by his tawny mane and massive neck, the male Steller's sea lion presides over his harem with an air of superiority and sovereignty, looking every bit the "lion of the sea." Numbers have been steadily declining in past decades.

Identifying Characteristics

Large body, tawny coat. With his thick neck and coarse mane, the adult male does resemble a lion.

Size: Males and females differ greatly in size: average male is nine feet, 1,500 pounds; females are generally seven feet, 600 pounds. Newborn pups are about three feet, 45 pounds.

Color: Blond to tawny beige, darker below. Newborns are dark brown.

Body: Large, robust body with broad, darker colored fore flippers and external earflaps. Male develops thickened neck and coarse mane. Muzzle is blunter and forehead is broader and flatter than with the California sea lion. Mouth curves down at corners.

Behavior: Adults growl and emit a low roar, but they do not bark continuously as do California sea lions.

Feeding: Opportunistic feeders, preying on a variety of fish, squid, and shrimp. Breeding males fast during mating season to retain territories; females feed between nursing bouts. It is estimated that they can dive to approximately 600 feet.

Social: Gregarious in haul-outs, but can be quite aggressive.

West Coast Range: Channel Islands to Alaska.
May Be Confused With: California sea lion.
Status: Listed as a "threatened species" on the Endangered Species List. There are about 100,000 to 116,000 worldwide. The Alaska population is about 64,000 and sharply declining. Native Alaskans hunt them for subsistence only, but commercial fishermen killed great numbers of Steller's during the 1970s and 1980s. Federal agencies have slowed this practice, but fisheries' interactions (including net entanglement) combined with other factors, such as disease and commercial overfishing of their prey, contribute to the downward population trend.

Commentary

The scientific community is directing its attention to the causes of the Steller's decline.

Northern fur seal

Scientific Name: *Callorhinus ursinus*
Family: Otariidae (The Eared Seals)

With its long black flippers and luxurious coat, this aristocrat among seals exudes elegance and style. Native peoples hunted them 10,000 years ago, and today they are hunted commercially in limited numbers for their beautiful skins.

Identifying Characteristics

Sleek fur. Small for an eared seal.

Size: Medium. Males are much larger than females, averaging 6.5 feet and 300 pounds compared to the average female, who is 4.2 feet and 70 to 110 pounds. Newborn pups are 2 feet long and 11 to 12 pounds.

Color: Fur may be silvery gray to brown. Fore flippers and hind flippers are black.

Body: Although small for an eared seal, they appear bulkier than sea lions. Fur seals have external earflaps and a rounded head with a conical muzzle. Ears are visible and are lower than eye level. Flippers are long, black, and leathery; hind flippers are greatly elongated to assist in grooming fur. Males develop thickened neck and mane.

Behavior: Northern fur seals are often seen far offshore, floating at the surface with their flippers arched over their bodies in a "jug handle" position. They spend a great deal of time rubbing their fur, which incorporates air bubbles that aid in heat retention. They often "porpoise" rapidly at the surface.

Feeding: Prey on schooling fish such as herring, capelin, and pollack, and small squid. Fur seals can dive to depths of over 600 feet for up to seven minutes.

Social: Spend most of the year far at sea but congregate in noisy, crowded rookeries at breeding and pupping time in midsummer. Reach sexual maturity at four to five years. Dominant males stake out and defend territories of receptive females. Pups nurse for around four months, and females leave their pups on shore to forage.

West Coast Range: Channel Islands to Alaska.

May Be Confused With: Guadalupe fur seal, Steller's sea lion.

Status: Owing to severe overexploitation, listed as a "depleted species" on the Endangered Species List. There are approximately 1.2 million throughout its range. Commercial harvests in the Pribilof Islands were not halted until 1984. Subsistence harvests now take fewer than 2,000 animals annually. Net entanglement contributes to their plight; pups are especially vulnerable.

Northern Fur Seal

Guadalupe fur seal

Scientific Name: *Arctocephalus townsendii*
Family: Otariidae (The Eared Seals)

Breeding only on remote volcanic Guadalupe Island off Mexico, the Guadalupe fur seal was hunted ruthlessly to presumed extinction in 1897. A few survived, however, and the species is making a slow recovery. Sometimes spotted in California's Channel Islands.

Identifying Characteristics

Small with sleek fur and a pointed snout.

Size: Small for an eared seal. There is considerable difference between adult males and females: males reach just over six feet and weigh about 350 pounds; females average four and a half feet and weigh around 100 pounds. The size of newborns remains unknown.

Color: Dark brown; may have lighter shading on chest.

Body: Small build, but thick fur coat adds bulk. Broad, leathery fore flippers and even longer hind flippers. Males develop a thickened neck mane. Head is distinctly pointed, with a sharply tapered collielike muzzle. External earflaps are set well back and low. Flippers are long, black, and leathery; hind flippers are greatly elongated for grooming fur.

Behavior: Prefer rocky habitats far offshore, but solitary fur seals may be encountered at sea.

Feeding: The remoteness of their habitat make this species difficult to study. Not much is known about feeding and diving behaviors, but it is assumed they feed on rockfish and squid, which are generally present in the areas they frequent.

Social: Solitary at sea, but gregarious in their preferred rocky haul-out areas. Sexual maturity probably occurs at four to five years. Pups are born in summer and, like other fur seal pups, probably remain with their mother for an extended period.

West Coast Range: Guadalupe Island off Baja California. A few animals have been recorded at the Channel Islands, and there have been recent sightings as far north as Monterey and the Farallon Islands off San Francisco.

May Be Confused With: Northern fur seal, California sea lion.

Status: Population is approximately 2,500 and increasing. They are not considered an endangered species because their remote habitat isolates them from any immediate threats by human or natural predators.

Sea Otter

Scientific Name: *Enhydra lutris*
Family: Mustelidae (The Weasels)

Sea otters have the densest fur of any animal on earth, a distinction that almost led to their extinction by fur traders.

Identifying Characteristics

Smallest marine mammal in region. Weasel-like body with a long, thick tail. Found close to shore in kelp beds and rocky shorelines. Typically swims on back with paws in the air.

Size: Male is about five feet long, and between 70 and 100 pounds. Female is about four feet long, 60 pounds. Newborns weigh about 5 pounds.

Color: Dark brown to blond; fur on head is paler. Heads and necks lighten with age, turning almost white.

Body: Webbed hind feet. Long flat tail that is very thick at base. Round head with small external ears. Retractable claws on front paws.

Behavior: Usually swim belly-up, front paws in the air. Using hind feet for propulsion, they swim at speeds of 2 to 3 mph. Roll to dive. Generally dive for one to two minutes but can stay down for five minutes. Frequently groom fur.

Feeding: Clams, sea urchins, abalone, crabs, mussels, starfish, fish. Otters eat at the surface of the water, using their chest as a "table," at times breaking their prey open against a rock held on the chest.

Social: "Raft" together in sexually segregated groups of up to several hundred animals.

West Coast Range: Aleutian Islands to southeast Alaska. Small transplanted populations in British Columbia, the northwest coast of Washington state, and in California from Santa Cruz to Pismo Beach.

May Be Confused With: River otter, pinnipeds.

Status: Protected and endangered. Sea otters are steadily recolonizing their former ranges in California and Alaska, but their sensitivity to environmental pollution, particularly oil spills, keeps them at risk.

READING
LIST

Bernard, Hannah, and Michele Morris. *The Oceanic Society Field Guide to the Humpback Whale.* Sasquatch Books, 1993.

Bonner, Nigel. *Whales of the World.* Facts On File Publications, 1989.

Channin, Paul. *The Natural History of Otters.* Facts On File Publications, 1985.

Connor, Richard C., and Dawn Micklethwaite Peterson. *The Lives of Whales and Dolphins.* Henry Holt & Co., 1994.

Cousteau, Jacques-Yves, and Yves Paccalet. *Whales.* Harry N. Abrams, 1986.

Evans, Peter G. H. *The Natural History of Whales and Dolphins.* Facts On File Publications, 1987.

Gordon, David G., and Alan Baldridge. *Gray Whales.* Monterey Bay Aquarium, 1991.

Harrison, Sir Richard J., and Dr. M. M. Bryden, eds. *Whales, Dolphins, and Porpoises.* Facts On File Publications, 1988.

Jefferson, Thomas A., Stephen Leatherwood, Marc A. Webber. *Marine Mammals of the World.* FAO, 1993.

King, Judith. *Seals of the World.* Cornell University Press, 1983.

Leatherwood, Stephen, and Randall R. Reeves. *The Sierra Club Handbook of Whales and Dolphins.* Sierra Club Books, 1983.

Love, John A. *Sea Otters.* Fulcrum Publishing, 1992.

Meyers, Susan. *Pearson, A Harbor Seal Pup.* Dutton, 1980.

Minasian, Stanley M., Kenneth C. Balcomb, Larry Foster. *The World's Whales.* Smithsonian Books, 1984.

Obee, Bruce, and G. Ellis. *Guardians of the Whales: The Quest to Study Whales in the Wild.* Alaska Northwest Books, 1992.

Oceanic Society. *The Oceanic Society Field Guide to the Gray Whale.* Sasquatch Books, 1989.

———. *Oceanic Society Field Guide to the Humpback Whale.* Sasquatch Books, 1993.

Orr, Robert. *Marine Mammals of California.* University of California Press, 1972.

Osborne, Richard, John Calambokidis, and Eleanor M. Dorsey. *A Guide to Marine Mammals of Greater Puget Sound.* Island Publishers, 1988.

Paine, Stefani. *The World of the Sea Otter.* Sierra Club Books, 1993.

Reeves, Randall R., Brent S. Stewart, and Stephen Leatherwood. *The Sierra Club Handbook of Seals and Sirenians.* Sierra Club Books, 1992.

Ridgeway, S., and Sir Richard J. Harrison. *Handbook of Marine Mammals.* Vol. 2, *Seals.* Academic Press, 1981.

Riedman, Marianne. *The Pinnipeds: Seals, Sea Lions, and Walrus.* University of California Press, 1990.

Riedman, Marianne. *Sea Otters.* Monterey Bay Aquarium, 1990.

Scammon, Charles M. *The Marine Mammals of the Northwestern Coast of North America, Together with an Account of the American Whale Fishery.* Dover, 1968. (Original 1874)

Scheffer, Victor B. *Little Calf.* Scribner, 1970.

Scheffer, Victor B. *The Year of the Seal.* Scribner, 1970.

Scheffer, Victor B. *The Year of the Whale.* Scribner, 1969.

Watson, Lyall. *Sea Guide to Whales of the World.* Dutton, 1981.

Wynne, Kate. *Guide to Marine Mammals of Alaska.* Alaska Sea Grant College Program, 1992.

INDEX